THE MIRACLE
One Musician's
Amazing Struggle for Survival

By Shelly Poole

First published 2011
Copyright @ Words HQ
The Helm
Carradale
Argyll
www.wordshq.co.uk

To Tony Barrell, my very talented writer friend. Thanks for your hours of hard work sifting through all of my emotional ramblings and turning The Miracle into what I hoped it would be. I couldn't have done it without you.

ONE morning in September 2009, 40-year-old Ally McErlaine – the lead guitarist in Texas, the famous Scottish rock band – was found unconscious at home, having stopped breathing after an enormous seizure. Doctors discovered that he had suffered a devastating brain haemorrhage, and said it was extremely unlikely that he would survive. Over the long months that followed, an extraordinary "rainbow army" of medical experts, alternative practitioners, religious devotees, spiritual healers and mystics joined forces with Ally's family and friends to achieve the impossible: bring Ally back to life.

THE MIRACLE tells the full story of this epic battle to save Ally. It reveals how this remarkable man defied the odds and returned from the dead. Told in intimate detail by his wife, the singer and songwriter Shelly Poole, this is an inspiring tale of love, tragedy and hope, and the chronicle of an event that challenges mainstream 21st-century science. It is a story that compels you to read to its amazing conclusion, while entertaining you with countless astonishing, heart-warming and humorous moments . . .
– And THE MIRACLE really did happen.

CHAPTER 1

THIS story really begins in Paris, in March 1996 at the Hôtel la Perle near Saint-Germain-des-Prés. I was 24 at the time, and in a band called Alisha's Attic with my elder sister, Karen. Kaz and I had put the band together when we were just 15 and 16, and set up shop in a loft in Barking, which belonged to the dad of our schoolfriend and co-songwriter Terry Martin.

Before Alisha's Attic, we'd been Astral Chime, Book of Dreams, and various other very badly named outfits with several very badly written songs – although of course we were convinced they were brilliant (we even had a song called 'Love Prevails, You've Got To Want It To!', with an exclamation mark!). We finally settled on the new name and honed the Alisha's sound, which consisted of beautiful harmonies and strange little hooky songs, crossing every genre.

Alisha's was our life, and we poured our hearts and souls into it. We'd eventually signed to Howard Berman at Mercury Records in the summer of 1995, and the following year we'd set off on a European trip to promote our first album, Alisha Rules the World. So we'd arrived in Paris for two days to appear on a TV show, and my life was just about to change.

The show turned out to be a ridiculous experience: Kaz and I had to walk down a big flight of stairs, which lit up with each footstep, to meet our backing band at the bottom. We then had to walk to our positions on stage while waving, to the accompaniment of a big-band intro, complete with trombones and timpanis. It wasn't quite the look we were going for then, so we did half an hour of moaning to our manager Paul White, about how we weren't 'wavers'.

Paul's nicknames for us then were Betty and Joan, after Davis and Crawford, and he mock-dramatically put the back of his hand to his forehead and mimicked our words in a funny American accent – 'Paul, we just *don't* wave!' Our aversion to waving is so funny to me now – I'd wave at anything and anyone today, because it just doesn't matter.

Anyway, we ended up complying because the singers Charles Aznavour and Jane Birkin, who I adored, were on the show too and they were doing it. By the time we got back to the Hôtel la Perle around 10 o'clock in the evening, we were in serious need of a drink.

It happened that the Scottish band Texas were staying at the same hotel: we were on the same label, Mercury Records, and you'd often find you were staying in the same place as your label-mates. The whole band were in the bar as we walked in. I saw their 27-year-old lead guitarist, Ally McErlaine, straight away: I remember thinking he was so very pretty and actually had the sparkliest green eyes I had ever seen.

I was probably instantly a little bit in love, although I'd never have admitted it, because I was fiercely independent and it wouldn't have been at all cool to do that.I'd never met Ally until then, though I'd met the lead singer, Sharleen Spiteri, a few times before. I'd had a conversation with her at a Christmas-carol event at the Union Chapel in Islington, where we'd discussed how hard it is to meet people and start relationships when you're constantly recording and touring in a band. And she'd mentioned Ally, and said how sweet he was and that he wasn't going out with anyone. Maybe, she said, Ally and I should hook up.

Everyone got talking over drinks that night in Paris, and four of us stayed up until four in the morning: Marcus, the guitarist in Alisha's Attic; Eddie, the keyboard player in Texas; and Ally and I. I know I was very drunk, because recalling most of the conversation we had that night is impossible, but I do remember being aware that Ally was very easy company: he was such an intelligent, unassuming, laid-back guy, so unlike what you would normally expect of a boy in a successful rock band.

When Marcus and I eventually excused ourselves, I gave both Ally and Eddie a kiss on the cheek, but we didn't arrange to meet again or anything like that. I remember Marcus saying 'I think Ally likes you,' but it all seemed very embarrassing and I brushed him off with a remark about not being able to understand a single word Ally said – he does have quite a strong Glaswegian accent. I also said something like 'But did you see his teeth? They're black!' What I didn't realize, until I got back to my room that night, was that all of us had black teeth from drinking all that Châteauneuf-du-Pape!

Secretly I was hoping I'd see Ally again really soon. And I didn't have to wait very long for that second encounter, because later that year we found ourselves sitting next to each other at the Irish music awards in Dublin. It turned out that the head of Mercury International, Sian Thomas, had deliberately seated us together because she was convinced we were made for each other. It was one of those really classic showbiz nights, speckled with funny moments that are all too rare in the music industry now. We were lucky enough to be at the tail end of a time when copious amounts of cash were spent on the artists and their art, and lavish parties were thrown.

Everyone partied hard, and there were plenty of 'characters' working for the record companies, some even more notorious than the artists themselves. It was a great time and I can only remember good and funny things about it. That night, the woman who was my publisher at the time became quite drunk and lost her shoe, and I remember her looking under all the tables on her hands and knees, and suddenly popping up between the legs of a very bemused Van Morrison.

A drunken radio DJ said he wanted to blow into my recorder, the wind instrument I always carried with me when we were performing, but Ally very chivalrously rescued me. He came straight over and said to the DJ: 'What are you doing with my wife?' I loved that, and it turned out to be prophetic. I had to fly early in the morning to Japan, where Kaz and I were doing a promotional trip, so I had to leave in a hurry and I didn't get to say goodbye.

Apparently, Ally left the awards with an awfully stiff neck, which meant that he had to wear a special collar for two weeks. This was the start of a long-term health problem, which still pains him to this day, and neither of us has any idea what caused it.Two Alisha's Attic singles were released and became big hits – I Am, I Feel, and Alisha Rules the World – and then Kaz and I went on a tour of Southeast Asia and

Australia. We flew back from Australia to attend the Brit Awards in London, because Alisha's Attic were one of the nominees.

That evening, I looked around the room, really hoping to see Ally, as I was in a posh frock for once. He wasn't there, but I spotted Texas's manager Gerry sitting at a nearby table. Quite unlike my usual self, I marched up to him, handed him my phone number and said: 'If Ally's ever in town, tell him to call me.' I explained that I was going back to finish off the tour in two days, so basically Ally needed to be quick if he wanted to see me in the next four months.

I was trying to be cool (it was only much later in life that I realized, after so much wasted effort, that there's really no hope of me being cool). There was no phone call – oh well – so we left to resume the tour and 'I Am, I Feeled' our way around Australia. But about two weeks later, Sian Thomas called our Australian hotel room to say that Ally was doing international press interviews on the phone from his Glasgow flat and that she was going to slot in a call to me at the end of the session. When Sian put him through, Ally explained that he had initially thought that Gerry was playing a joke on him with the phone number. (They were always playing practical jokes on each other: once, he informed Ally that when he first arrived across the English border, he had to go into the petrol station and show his passport – and hilariously, Ally followed his instructions to the letter!)

Eventually, when he had a rare moment alone, Ally had decided to give the number a go, what the hell. He had gone to a public telephone box in London's Russell Square, which he knew was just round the corner from the flat I shared with Karen. If I had answered, the plan was for him to come round to see me. But part of him still suspected that Gerry was 'having a laugh' and it was the number of a Chinese restaurant or something, and he said he was genuinely shocked when he heard my voice on the answering machine. So shocked, in fact, that after leaving a brief nervous message he'd walked off, leaving his wallet with about £300 and all his credit cards (and my phone number) in the phone box. Of course, when he finally realized what he had done and rushed back, his wallet was long gone. I've since told myself that I should have seen this as a warning of disasters to come.

Since the Russell Square phone-box incident, Ally has managed to leave his property everywhere. He has gone out for whole days and left ground-floor sash windows wide open, driven off after leaving a shoe box on the roof of the car, actually lost his car... I could go on and on, but this is coming from the girl who once took a letter and a purse to the postbox, posted the purse and returned home with the letter! I think Sian was spot-on: we were made for each other.

Anyway, during that phone call we arranged to meet three weeks later, when I flew back from Australia for the Capital music awards. It was our first official date.

The awards were another brilliant music-industry occasion. We spent a lot of time with Michael Hutchence and the boys in INXS, as Alisha's Attic were just about to support them on tour. I'd holidayed with Michael and Paula Yates the previous summer at Dave Stewart's house in the South of

France, so we were friends already. It was such an exciting notion to go on tour with INXS – they were a fantastic band – and we were planning all the social events, like tenpin bowling, that we were going to enjoy together.

Ally and I were stuck together like glue that night: we're together in every photograph I have of the event. Even in the one where I'm sitting on the lap of the England goalkeeper Peter Shilton, comparing his huge hands against mine, Ally has his fingers behind my head like bunny ears. That was the night that my big sister met Ally: Karen said he was gorgeous and she totally approved (which was a first), and Ally and I held hands for the first time as we walked around Mayfair. I was due to go away again in the morning, Texas were off on tour, and it was going to be hard to separate this time.One evening after we'd reunited again, Ally came over to my London flat for beans on toast (he had the ones that come with mini sausages and I didn't, because I'm a vegetarian).

While we were enjoying this wondrous meal, we had a slightly awkward conversation that finally cemented our relationship. 'Are you my boyfriend?' I asked. He said: 'Well, I don't know. Do you want me to be?' I replied: 'Well, do you want to be?' We ended up with a big fat 'yes' and were both so glad that we'd had this major 'discussion' and made it all official.

Ally and I had been together for about four years when we were invited to Alaska, of all places, for a fabulous party being thrown by Paul Allen, who co-founded Microsoft with Bill Gates. The party was on a ship, and just after we'd docked at the city of Juneau, a bunch of us wandered into a diamond shop. Ally was eyeing up the watches while the women were looking at the rings and other sparkly things.

Really loudly and completely out of the blue, our make-up artist and friend, Debbie Bunn, suggested that Ally get me an engagement ring, which led to another of those awkward conversations.

Ally turned to me and asked: 'Do you want one?' To which I said: 'Well, I don't know. Do you want to buy me one?' He replied: 'If you want one, yes.'   'I want one,' I decided.

'Okay, then. We're engaged,' he announced. It took us three years to actually get round to the wedding.

I had an unheard-of day off, plus a few weeks coming up that weren't too busy, and I suddenly got the urge. I phoned Ally, who was sitting on a tour bus somewhere with Texas, and said 'Can we get married next month?'

He said, 'If you can book it and turn it all around in a day, yes!' So I phoned the register office in Glasgow where Ally said he'd like to get married, and I booked us in for four weeks later, October 5, 2001 – it so happened there was a lucky cancellation! – and then I phoned everyone I loved and gave them the date.

I booked the Arthouse Hotel, where Sharleen's sister Corrine worked: we'd stayed there many times and knew the food was amazing. I booked 100 lunches, and 15 bedrooms for my London lot. I bought my dress and shoes in a vintage shop the day before, and Ally didn't even wear a tie. There were no place settings on the tables – we all just piled in. It was perfect. I'd always thought that being the kind of girl I am,

I'd go for a real movie-star romance, with a suave David Niven type. My dad has often said that I always do the opposite of what's expected: if there's an easy road, I'll always take the hard one.

With Ally, I definitely chose the opposite of what everybody expected – including me. But I knew for certain that Ally and I were made for each other. You can see the evidence in the photographs taken on our wedding day: there we are, outside the register office in Park Circus, Glasgow, surrounded by all our friends and family, confetti flying everywhere.

I'm in a vintage 1950s-style Doris Day wedding dress (which was accidentally tucked into my knickers) and Ally has a cigarette in one hand, while his other hand was making those bloody bunny ears behind my head again.

CHAPTER 2

THE Noughties brought some interesting changes for Ally and me. Karen and I had decided to bring Alisha's Attic to an end after our third album in 2001. We knew it was for the best – we'd taken the band as far as it could go – but it was like saying goodbye to an old friend.

All my funniest, happiest, saddest, strangest and most wondrous times happened in the world of Alisha's Attic, and I still miss those times madly – but without ever wanting them back, paradoxically.

In the world of music publishing, you're sent 'tip sheets' that tell you about artists looking for songs, and we saw a lot of tip sheets saying things like 'Quirky artist on Warner's, needing songs like Alisha's Attic', or 'Girl-band member starting solo career, looking for songs in the vein of Alisha's Attic'. I decided I could write those songs, so in addition to branching out as a solo artist, I started writing for other singers. Since then I've worked with some of the best in the business, and had a blast doing it. Meanwhile, with Texas on a long hiatus, Ally was writing some beautiful guitar music and also taking up photography in a big way.

He adored taking pictures. We'd be just about to sit dowand watch television for the evening, and he'd grab his camera and say: 'Shell, can you stand in that doorway with a lampshade on your head?' or 'Shell, can you put your face in this transparent bucket of water, and open your eyes and look towards the lens?' He was constantly curious about how things looked, and wanted to capture a kind of visual truth, and I'd always oblige. Ally had been experimenting with the world and making art since he was a boy. As a nine-year-old schoolboy, he'd draw the most graphic and lifelike pictures on his exercise books: terrifying images of men having their arms cut off and eyes gouged out, with blood spurting everywhere. I've seen his maths book, and it's a total horror story.

All that stuff might be connected to the fact he was born on October 31 – Hallowe'en. He told me he'd always associated birthdays with ghosts and monsters, because that's what he'd dress up as on every birthday. He liked his own company, and would spend hours alone in his bedroom in his parents' rented high-rise flat, where he'd play guitar, listen to Rush records and carry out his own slow nature experiments: he'd put water in a jar and add some other found organic matter to it, and then leave it to see what kind of fungus grew, or what other metamorphosis would occur.

I'm pleased he grew out of this habit – although, having said that, I remember that on one of our first dates, in his flat above an electrical shop on the South Side of Glasgow, we spent the whole evening digging things out of the sink and looking at them under his microscope. I remember him saying how funny it would be if these things could see us, and watch how we spent our time. It was if he was looking at the world through the wrong end of the microscope.

In 2001 we started going on walking and climbing holidays in Scotland with a group of friends. They were nothing to do with music, and it was so refreshing to get away and explore the beautiful unspoiled wilds of the Highlands with these people, who taught us so much about nature and opened our eyes to the beauty of it. This is when Ally became fascinated with macro photography – taking close-up pictures of things and revealing an incredible amount of detail.

On high climbs we would suddenly lose him in the long grass, and he would get himself into the weirdest positions as he pointed his camera at natural forms to create images that looked like miniature landscapes or the surface of the moon. He was continually snapping, and the world looked fantastic through that lens, but I'd moan at him sometimes to put the camera down and start looking at things through his own human eyes!

Two years ago, our very dear friends Holly and Bradley had a child, and because baby Freddie had never seen Ally's face from behind the lens, they nicknamed him 'Uncle Nikon'. I think Freddie still thinks Ally's got a hard plastic rotating nose! Ally loved reading science books and regaling me with fascinating fact after fascinating fact. When we were in bed, he'd read out stuff about the universe, and tell me about the countless incredible things that exist out in space, and then I'd lie there thinking about it all, unable to sleep. But where Ally is a very rational thinker, and tends to believe there's a scientific equation to explain everything, I've always had more ethereal tendencies.

I was on the hippie trail when I met Ally – trying out every religion going, on a spiritual quest for something. As a child, I'd get up in the morning and tell my mum 'I'm a Hindu today,' and she'd smile and say: 'Oh, lovely, dear.' One day I decided to be a Catholic (a girl had brought a book in to school of all the saints – she said they looked after her, and I wanted them to look after me too), so I told Mum I was going to be a nun.

She did a good job of putting me off by telling me that you have to give up your vanity, so all of your hair had to be cut really short. So how was it, I asked Mum, that Julie Andrews had such good hair in The Sound of Music? She replied with the bombshell that she wasn't a real nun: she was acting, just pretending to be one. Oh, the horror: Julie Andrews, a bogus nun? Needless to say, by the following morning I was a Buddhist. Early on in our relationship, I noticed that Ally was brilliant at sourcing music to listen to; he'd spend hours scouting all over the place for new and interesting things to fill his ears. And one day in 2007, as we drove towards Regents Park in London on a beautiful afternoon, he played me an amazing song on the stereo – Marry Song, by Band of Horses – which I instantly adored and found really inspiring. I played it over and over again, while my thoughts started kicking something about.

Sometimes moments happen and you recognize them as the start of something, and listening to those boys singing in the car that day was truly a 'moment'. In 2008 we moved into a dormer bungalow in Muswell Hill. It's a funny little house built in the 1940s, raised up above street level in the middle of a road full of Victorian terraced houses.

It seems totally out of place, and looks like it should be by the seaside in Southend, which is exactly why we bought it. One day, Ally and I were both working separately on some music at home in the bungalow, as we often do. Ally was upstairs in the studio with all his guitars plugged in, and I was downstairs with my laptop computer at the dining-room table, working on some lyrics for a Westlife song.

Suddenly he emailed me with a piece of music he had just written, which he labelled 'pretty thing'. After it pinged into my inbox, I put it straight into my recording program, turned my microphone on and started singing along.

I love writing like that: just plugging the mic in and singing as the music plays, so you don't know any of the chord changes, can make for the most unusual melodies and phrasing. Out came this tune, Morning Song, all done and dusted in the space of an hour. The song has a beautiful two-part harmony all the way through, and I love harmonies.

My dad, Brian Poole, was the singer with the 1960s band The Tremeloes, and so much of the music that Dad had played to Kaz and me as kids in the 1970s had amazing harmonies: the Eagles, the Doobie Brothers and Simon and Garfunkel were our staple diet as we drove around London in Dad's Ford Mustang, looking up at all the enormous mansions in The Bishops Avenue and imagining how I was going to live in one of those when I grew up. As a child I'd sing the descant parts in the church choir, and at home Kaz and I would sing every Abba song in perfect two-part harmony.

Harmonies were later a big part of the Alisha's Attic sound, too, and I'd missed hearing them, and the way they make the world feel good for a minute or two. We recorded a rough demo of Morning Song, with me singing both harmonies. But to record it properly, we felt we needed another voice for the harmony. Initially we thought of Jack Savoretti, who is a singer-songwriter I've worked with and rate very highly. But Ally thought the all-female demo sounded magical, so we decided we needed a female singer.

A while back, I'd been called in to write songs with a singer who had the curious name of Charity Hair. Charity was in a band called The Ailerons with my friend Dave Rowntree, the drummer from Blur, and she has an amazing voice. She is American and has that country twang, although she was doing everything to hide it at the time. So I called Charity, sent her the demo and asked if she'd sing on the recording, and she immediately said yes, she'd love to. When the three of us got together and played, it was so exciting. I actually cried when I heard Charity singing the vocal on Morning Song. At that point, we decided to form a band together – a band that would exist purely to satisfy our own selfish musical needs. We'd only write stuff we loved, and we wouldn't care if it didn't fit anywhere in the scheme of modern commercial music.

Everything we did in the rest of our working lives was a compromise – it always had to please someone else – so this would be a fantastic antidote to all of that. In bed one night, I thought of a name for the band; I mentioned it to Ally, but couldn't be bothered to get out of bed and write it down. He said if I remembered it in the morning, then that was the name.

Charity called early the next morning, and I said 'Ooh, I've got something to tell you… Oh blimey, what is it?… What is it… Oh! Red Sky July.' I didn't even have to say '… is a band name I was thinking of', because she said 'That's a perfect band name. Let's have it!' So we brought in a musician pal, Mark Neary, and a producer friend, Graeme Pleeth, and started recording in earnest. And in June 2009, Red Sky July acquired a manager – Jazz Summers, who'd managed the Verve and Wham! – and we were all incredibly chuffed. It meant we could have a bit of funding to finish our album the way we really wanted to. We were all set to record in Bristol from October 3, with Rory Carlisle producing.

For the first time in ages, we were feeling really excited about our music and our future. As far as we knew, Ally and I were both healthy as well as happy. Okay, he was carrying a little extra weight at the time, but he was going regularly to the gym to rectify that. Ally's dad had had two heart attacks in his late fifties, so I was worried about Ally putting on weight, but he was a grown man and he said he was doing all he could, and I believed him.

A few years earlier, he'd visited the doctor complaining of a sore throat, and he'd been examined and told he had high blood pressure. Rather than take pills for it, he told the doctor he'd look at his diet. Unlike me, he hasn't been a staunch vegetarian for most of his life, and doesn't abstain from tea and coffee. He'd given up smoking after our wedding, which I was enormously pleased about. But I kept finding empty crisp packets and sweet wrappers stuffed in secret places around the house0. We didn't think anything of it when, one day while we were recording at Graeme's house, Ally complained of a headache. It was bad enough for him to ask for painkillers, which he took, and the headache went away.

On the beautiful, balmy evening of Monday, September 7, 2009, Ally and I wandered home after spending some time with Mark Neary at our local pub, the Maid of Muswell. We were in the process of selling our house in Muswell Hill, and we were talking about the good offer we'd received that day on it from a guy out of Eastenders: we decided to accept it.

Also, we discussed the idea of having kids – something we hadn't talked about before – and decided that yes, it was a good time to think about doing that. Loads of people had careers and babies, so why shouldn't we? He piggybacked me home as if we were a pair of kids, and we got into our lovely big oak bed and went off to sleep half an hour past midnight. Both of us were extremely happy – almost dazed with contentment about how life was treating us – and really looking forward to what tomorrow would bring.

CHAPTER 3

I WOKE up around 8.30 on the morning of Tuesday, September 8, to the most disturbing noise I'd ever heard, like the very loud emptying of a huge drain. Ally was always up before me, and he'd put the kettle on, so I usually woke up to that. I called out to him, but he didn't answer. I called again – nothing. Suddenly a strange dread came over me, an eerie feeling that something was terribly wrong.

I ran out of the bedroom, and from behind the front-room door I saw his feet hanging over the edge of the sofa. They were totally still. I dashed into the front room and found him lying on the sofa the way he often does, but his eyes were rolled back into his head, his tongue was hanging out, and his skin had turned a horrible grey colour. I was terrified, and nothing I did seemed to have any effect. I shouted at him, punched him, and prised his eyes open with my trembling hands – but he just wasn't there. The drain-like noise had stopped now: it had been the sound of him trying to breathe, and he wasn't doing that any more. There was a deathly silence instead. I ran around the house in a panic, searching for the cordless phone. When I found it, I suddenly couldn't remember the emergency number. What was it? 911? 999! That was it.

The wonderful man on the other end of the line gave me instructions: he asked me to try to move Ally so that he was lying flat. I tried that, but by this time he was a dead weight; his whole body had apparently shut down, which meant he was covered in piss and shit. And I couldn't get my fingers down his throat to clear his airways, as the man told me to do, because his head was propped up against the arm of the sofa. All I could think to do was punch his chest, which was such an awful thing to do. I remember screaming down the phone 'He's not breathing! Oh my God, he's not breathing!'

About seven minutes later, a paramedic arrived and asked me to help him lift Ally off the sofa and place him on the floor.

I held Ally's feet while the paramedic held his shoulders, but it was a real struggle. Five other paramedics arrived, and they surrounded Ally on the floor; I couldn't see what they were doing. I phoned my dad and told him what had happened, and he asked lots of questions I couldn't answer. It was all happening too quickly.

'Get him breathing, get him breathing!' I screamed at the paramedics, and finally one of them replied 'Okay, he's breathing.' Dad said he'd get straight into his car and drive over. Meanwhile I stared in horror at the walls, which were covered in the blood and gunge that Ally had vomited up while they were trying to resuscitate him on our Persian rug.

The paramedics put Ally on a stretcher and carried him into the back of the ambulance. One of them told me to get dressed quickly, so he could take me in a car and we'd follow the ambulance to the Whittington Hospital, between Archway and Highgate.

I kept thinking that Ally didn't have any clothes on, and how he would have hated that, being carried naked into the street. Reality had turned into a kind of slow-motion dream. For a while I was alone in the hospital waiting room, and then a doctor came in with that look you see on Casualty and a thousand other hospital dramas.

'I'm afraid we can't say yet what's happened to your husband,' he told me. 'We think it's some kind of seizure.' He said the word as if it was useful and informative, but it was just confusing – what exactly had he been seized by?

He explained that Ally was on a life-support machine, which was now doing his breathing for him. Would I like to see him?

They pulled back the curtains. Everything was so still and he looked as if he was dead. But I kissed him, talked to him, and wiped a bit of blood off his lip.

Dad and Mum arrived, and so did my sister Karen and her husband Dave, who had brought me clothes to wear, as I hadn't dressed properly and I was still covered in Ally's bodily fluids. I took Dad in to see Ally, and realized how suddenly calm I was: actually, I felt completely numb, just waiting for the next set of instructions to follow.

Within an hour of arriving at the Whittington, there was a surgeon waiting for Ally in the National Hospital for Neurology

& Neurosurgery, which is in Queen Square in Bloomsbury – not far from where I used to live. The doctor seemed really pleased about getting him a place in the hospital, so I was pleased too and thanked him. Seven people travelled with Ally and all his machinery in an ambulance, and we all followed behind it: me, Mum and Dad, Kaz and Dave. We were all in a dreamlike state.

Dad and I ran through the doors of the National Hospital. We were alone, as Mum and Dave wanted to go back to the house and clear up the signs of what had happened. It was an awful mess, and I didn't really want them to have to do that, but they were adamant. I had this terrible vision – it was all I could think of – of our front-room walls covered in bits of my husband, like a Jackson Pollock painting. We couldn't find Ally, and we were getting desperate. It was so strange to be without him and not know where he was – I hated that.

Eventually a doctor sat us down in the basement, where the operating theatre was, and told us that he'd been taken in to emergency surgery, where they were trying to find out exactly what had happened to him. If they confirmed what they suspected, that he'd had some kind of brain seizure, they might be able to operate on him then and there, depending on the scale of the problem and the part of the brain that had been affected.

They told me it wasn't looking good, which I knew anyway. I signed the risk forms they gave me, and Dad and I did what we were told and waited for five hours while they operated on Ally.

We went to the chapel in the hospital and prayed and prayed, and dad cried out loudly to God, 'Why didn't you take me instead, you bastard?' We kept checking the waiting room nervously for any signs of the surgeons who were trying to save Ally. Six-and-a-half hours of surgery later, a friendly silver-haired doctor took Dad and me into a tiny room on the first floor by the critical-care unit.

At this point, we still had absolutely no idea what was going on. 'Ally has had a grade-5 subarachnoid brain haemorrhage,' said the doctor, 'which is the largest bleed. It's all over the brain, not just one area, and has been devastating to him. I'm so sorry.'

The haemorrhage was the result of an aneurysm, caused by a weakness in one of the blood vessels in his brain. I was in shock and couldn't breathe. Dad and I just stared at each other. I was asked if he'd taken any drugs (no, of course not, he'd never been into drugs) and a lot of other questions about his lifestyle. I said that we'd been in the pub the night before and he'd had two glasses of wine, and he hadn't felt at all poorly.

I was asked if he'd gone off to the loo on his own at any time, or if he could have been taking drugs without my knowledge. No! Absolutely not. I know my husband!

The surgeon who'd worked on Ally came in next, and told us that he had managed to coil the aneurysm – which is a way of blocking the weak artery that had caused the seizure, and cutting it off from the blood supply with lots of tiny aluminium coils. To carry out this procedure, they go right up the arterial veins in the groin. Because of the sheer amount of blood, he'd initially suspected that Ally may have had multiple aneurysms, but he could only find one, at the back of the brain, in the middle.

'This is good, right?' I wondered to myself. Unfortunately, they have to tell you the statistics: 96% of grade-5 patients die before they reach the hospital, and the rest usually die within the first four days, or on the onset of what they call vasospasms – the condition in which blood vessels spasm and become constricted.

'This is what we expect to happen,' he went on. 'After such a trauma, usually within the next 24 to 48 hours the brain swells, and this can be fatal.' They gave us two other horrific scenarios and then finished with the vasospasm speech: they can't really treat that, as they don't know why it happens. I couldn't really take any more in. They told us the situation was hopeless: 'Ally is certain to die. Please get close family here as soon as possible, as we don't expect him to last the night.' I looked at Dr Silverhair, who I knew did this every day, and said 'My husband wouldn't leave me like this, I just know it. I can't explain it, but I just know this isn't his fate.' But he held my hand and told Dad we should really start looking at funeral arrangements.

Nothing can ever prepare you for something like this. On that horrible day, I wrote these stark words in my diary:

Normal life stops… Found ally 8.30 on the sofa Aneurysm grade 5… They've told us he will die… I want to die.

That evening, Mum and our best friend, Steve Daniel, picked up Ally's mum and dad, Brenda and Alistair, from Stansted Airport. They'd flown from Glasgow and they were beside themselves with shock at what had happened. It was typical of Steve to be there when we needed him. He'd been my accountant when I was in Alisha's Attic; he'd bought my first flat and my first car for me. He'd quickly become Ally's best friend in London while I'd been away on a trip to Japan in 1997, and on our wedding day Steve had been there to drive me, Dad and our bridesmaids to the register office.

Back at the hospital, Ally's nurse told us it was okay to see him, so we entered the critical-care ward known as SITU (surgical intensive treatment unit), and there he was in a corner bed by the window.

He was just lying there, with his head shaved on one side and a tube down his throat. He was on life support, flatlined and not doing anything for himself. There were no signs of life at all, except for the beeping of the machines he was wired to – he was surrounded by so many contraptions, it looked as if he was in an alien aircraft. I just stood and stared at him in disbelief. But at least he looked peaceful, I thought.

Around 1am they asked us to leave, saying they'd phone us straight away if they needed us. I had the terrible feeling that he might die that night, and I found it so hard to leave him, but they insisted we go home and get some rest. Brenda and Alistair moved in to the spare room of our bungalow. Mum and Dave had done a fantastic clean-up job: the walls were all spotless, the rug was drying out in the darkness of the garden, and the sofa cushions were drying on the dining-room floor.

But I hated walking around the house that night: in my mind, I could still see Ally lying on the sofa with me on top of him, trying to thump his heart into beating again. I could still see all the paramedics crowding around him, and his body pumping away as they tried to resuscitate him, and I could still see the awful state of the house when I'd left it that morning. In our bedroom, Ally's cup was still on the bedside table from the night before, and his mobile phone was still on charge.

I didn't know 'sad' felt like this. I looked out of the bedroom window, dropped to my knees and cried like I'd never cried before, with no sound except the hiss of one long outward breath.

My diary for that day ends:

National Hospital of Neurology and Neurosurgery... Now in critical intensive care on life support... Not looking good but I still don't believe it... In a coma with tube down throat, looking serene and beautiful... They tell us 3 worst-case scenarios in a locked room... He's basically gone forever.

CHAPTER 4

I THOUGHT I'd find it really hard to sleep that night, but in fact I slept as if I'd been hit over the head with a baseball bat. I had a very vivid dream, and woke up with all the intense feelings from it. There were about 20 of us running really fast down a dusty road with mountains on either side, and Ally and I were out in front. It was almost a flying dream: our feet were floating above the ground and we got a great speed up.

Suddenly I realized Ally had fallen behind and I couldn't see him, and all the others were waving their arms at me to come back. I tried to stop, but it was hard, so I dug my heels into the ground, kicking up lots of dust, and turned to run back, but suddenly my legs weren't working properly: it took a huge amount of effort to move them.

The others were all crouching around something, and I looked between them to see Ally on the ground, with only half of his head. The other half was in my hand. I fell down next to him and tried desperately to fit the bit of skull back on, but it wouldn't fit. His eyes looked dead, everything was covered in blood and I was screaming but without making any sound.

We got up at six the next morning, dressed hurriedly, and Dave drove Ally's parents and me back to the National Hospital for Neurology & Neurosurgery. It was just a half-hour ride but it seemed like a lifetime.

My stomach was full of butterflies and I couldn't stop wondering – and dreading – what we'd find when we arrived. That day, I was supposed to be working with the songwriter Sheppard Solomon and a guy from the band Empire of the Sun, writing a song for a new girl band who were a bit like the Corrs. But I'd phoned my music publisher, Celia McCamley, and told her I needed to cancel all my work for the foreseeable future. She'd told me not to worry, and said I just had to take everything day by day. I'd normally have been mortified about cancelling work, but it wasn't bothering me at all then: everything I'd normally worry about had gone out the window.

I didn't care what I looked like, what the house looked like, or who was going to pay the bills: I thought about nothing except for Ally right then. I was in a bubble where I didn't eat, held my breath, and lived with a knot in my stomach that was the size of America.

Brenda and I weren't allowed to go in and see Ally straight away. We finally got in around 7.45am, after obsessively applying antibacterial solution to our hands and arms. Only two people were allowed round the bed at one time here in critical care, and you could see they didn't even like that, because they needed full access to the patient at all times. When the door opened, all the nurses and doctors spun round and gave us a look that could have been disapproval or pity, or a mixture of the two. But they'd have to get used to us being around, because we weren't going anywhere. The room was silent except for the beeping of machinery.

Suddenly the curtains were pulled all round Ally's bed, there was some frantic bashing about, and we were told that he wasn't doing well, so we had to sit in the waiting room for an hour while they tried to stabilize him. So we took up residence in the waiting room, and meanwhile the rest of the family arrived – Mum, Dad and Karen. Kaz was eight months pregnant, and not finding it easy to get around. And there was Steve with our other great friends Big Paul and Sandra, who Ally and I had met when we lived in a flat in Hampstead – we'd all lived within a few streets of each other. Since then we'd become a kind of unorthodox little London family, spending our birthdays and most of our holidays together.

All we could do was wait and wait, and from time to time Brenda and I would urge each other to go and peep through the small window in the surgery door to see if the staff were done with him yet, but the curtains stayed drawn for what seemed forever.

Eventually the head nurse in critical care came out, and our hearts sank as she asked us all to sit down and gave us the latest news. Quietly and gently, she told us that Ally's brain had swollen during the night.

Worse, it was still swelling at such a rate that they'd have to take him into surgery again that afternoon. It would be dangerous, she warned: there was a serious risk that he'd suffer a stroke or we'd lose him completely. Because of the risks, I had to sign another form. Dad asked her some questions – we'd decided between us that one of us should ask the questions and the other should take in the answers, because we had to know what Ally's chances were but there was an enormous amount of information to deal with.

Unfortunately, I could hardly take anything in: there was this blizzard of unfamiliar medical terms, and I was still locked in a slow-motion nightmare.

Ally had fluid on the brain, and they would have to put in a drain, because the brain was so damaged that it couldn't drain itself. And I remember being told that they'd try everything they could, but that I had to start being 'realistic'. And all we could do now was wait… and wait… and wait…

When Ally finally came out of surgery, Brenda and I went straight to see him. The drain they'd put in looked like a metal bolt and spring fixed to the right-hand side of his skull. He had a temperature of 41C and his blood pressure was sky-high, 210 over 114. I heard the staff talking about pneumonia, and every 20 minutes they had to use suction to remove the fluid on his lungs, which made the most awful sound and was grim to watch. His body was shaking, and every now and then it would fold in half as he vomited up lots of green stuff. This seemed to be the result of various infections he was suffering, and every time it happened we were ushered out of surgery.

Despite this sea of green that came out of his body in waves, he was still in a coma, and they couldn't detect any signs of brain activity. We couldn't hold either of his hands, because each one had about a dozen tubes leading from it, so we touched his face gently and I began talking to him.

At first I whispered close to his ear: 'Oh God, Ally, if you can hear me, concentrate on my voice and stay with it. Don't leave me, Ally! Please fight!' Then I started conversing with him as if we were together on a normal day, telling him how big Kaz was getting and how the baby had been kicking around inside her; how his mum and dad would be staying over at the bungalow till he was all better; and so-and-so had a new album out, and I'd bring it for him to listen to tomorrow.

Underneath all this small talk, I was thinking about how I really missed him, and couldn't bear the idea of living without him. Next to Ally was a big bag of brain fluid, which was bright red with blood. The heart monitor was making Morse-code-like beeps, and every time there was a long continuous one, it was so unnerving that Brenda and I ducked as if there'd been a gunshot. Then we'd be bustled out quickly as they tried to stabilize Ally again. And we'd wait some more and then come back in, the whole process repeating itself every 20 minutes. It was hideous.

At the end of the day, the lovely silver-haired doctor entered the room where we'd all gathered, locked the door and pulled the visor down over the little surgery viewing window. I still remember the sound of that visor coming down: it was something I came to dread, because it was the signal for a serious chat.

He sat down and told us all the terrifying truth: Ally was so severely brain-damaged, he couldn't keep his body properly regulated by himself. His heart rate just wouldn't come down –

when I looked at the heart monitor it showed a rate of 144, and I later discovered on the internet that the average resting heart rate for his age group was 71 to 75 – so there was a very high risk of cardiac arrest.

They still weren't sure if his brain was actually alive: by now, they'd have liked to see some signs of him biting down on the life-support tube, but he hadn't done that. They were still monitoring the swelling of his brain, and it hadn't gone down, though the fluid was being successfully drained.

If Ally is brain-dead, said Dr Silverhair, he's gone and there is nothing they can do. At some point, they'd try to bring him round and see what brain activity there was, which would tell them more. But whatever happens, he said, Ally would be severely brain-damaged. He explained the severely reduced quality of life Ally would have if he lived through this, how he'd need constant care and attention, and though he didn't use that awful word, it came into my head at this point.

He was telling me that if Ally got through this he'd be a vegetable, and that I had to start being realistic about that. He wouldn't be able to walk, wash or dress himself, eat for himself, let alone play guitar. Mentally, he'd be unlikely to know even who I was. It was just too awful to contemplate. I thanked the doctor, saying I was so grateful for his expertise and was so glad Ally had him working on him.

'But,' I asked, 'have you every known anyone to live through this?' He thought for a while, then said yes, there had been one person, in his many years of experience, who'd survived this – but she hadn't walked out of here.

'Great, that's all I need to know,' I told him. 'You don't know my husband, doctor – he won't let that happen to him. Just wait!' The way he looked at me when I said this, I could see he was really worried for me. But I knew how fiercely competitive Ally had always been. Although outwardly he would sometimes seem lazy and fatalistic, even defeatist, he was actually the most determined person I'd ever met. I remember Sharleen Spiteri saying how everyone would always think 'Ah, sweet Ally,' but how he was secretly as stubborn as a mule and would always get what he wanted.

In the many hours we'd spent at the hospital, I'd seen two families being told that their loved ones had died, and I'd seen the horror and disbelief on their faces. I saw a grief-stricken teenager sliding down a wall as his father tried to make him stand up, and a man and his daughter wandering aimlessly around the building, not knowing what to do next, as a body bag was wheeled into the lift.

But I felt that as long as Ally was lying next door with that big machine breathing for him, there was still hope. He was still on the planet and anything could happen; it was all in the balance, the luck of the draw.

After Dr Silverhair left, there was a lot of very sombre conversation in the waiting room, as we tried to penetrate all the medical jargon and establish what Ally's chances really were. There was basically no hope at all: he was so severely brain-damaged, he couldn't even breathe for himself. I went in with Dad to talk to Ally again. Though I had no idea whether he could hear me, I told him how his tomato plants were growing back home. Then Dad did some magic over Ally's head: he grasped the air, symbolically stealing the bad bits away from his brain; then, keeping his fist closed as tightly as possible, he went out of the room, opened his hand and let it go.

Dad and I had always believed in magic, and in the power of positive thinking. Once, when I was little and we were living in Barking in Essex, my mum lost the face from her watch. She loved that watch, and it was in the shape of a flower, so the face would've been very hard to replace. They'd looked everywhere for it, left no stone unturned, but it had just vanished. Times were hard for our family back then, and I remember wishing so hard that this lost thing would show itself to me, so I could return it to Mum and make her happy.

Shortly afterwards, I stood on a wicker chair to reach a cream-cracker tin on a shelf, and when I jumped down and put the chair back, there it was – tiny but clearly illuminated by the sun, tucked into the wickerwork of the chair where it must have fallen: the lost watch face. I ran and told Dad what I'd done and how it had worked, but he wasn't the slightest bit shocked. 'Of course it works, darling,' he said quite matter-of-factly. 'You can make anything happen if you wish hard enough.'

After Dad had performed his magic, I did some more serious talking to Ally. 'Don't you dare give up now, Ally,' I told him. 'You've fought too hard. Don't you bloody dare.'

One by one, we went and kissed him good-night, all of us praying inside that we wouldn't get that phone call in the middle of the night.

On that day, September 9, I wrote in my diary:

Still in coma... The brain started to swell as they said it might. Worst case 1 – they put a plug in his head and keep monitoring it. If it doesn't go down the options are shocking – not gonna write it down. He's stable but they say he's dying. On life support, no signs of life.

It's not good. Fuck fuck fuck...

CHAPTER 5

THERE was no phone call during the night, so we knew on the morning of Day 3 that Ally was still with us. But now I discovered that my sister Karen had taken the crisis very badly. From what I had overheard – because nobody wanted to tell me and give me something else to worry about – she had become emotional to the extent that she'd been hyperventilating, and had been taken to hospital because there were concerns about the baby.

This was supposed to be the happiest time for us all – the beginning of a new generation of the family – but there was no joy, only heartache. Karen hadn't actually seen Ally in hospital yet, as it would have been too distressing in her state, and I suggested she stay away for the time being, at least until we had a better idea of what was happening. We agreed that she and Dave would drive us to Bloomsbury on most days, so she'd still have an important role to play. That was actually a massive help: there was now way I could have driven – I couldn't even see straight. During the journey in one day, Kaz gave me a newspaper clipping about Richard Hammond, the Top Gear presenter who'd suffered a serious brain injury and had been in a coma after crashing a jet-powered car in 2006.

Ally's condition was actually more serious, but the clipping was inspiring because it said that when Richard was in the coma, he felt as if there were two roads he could take: the easy one, where he could drift off to 'sleep' and just give up, or the really hard one, where he had to fight and stay alive.

If Ally's brain was alive, I was sure he'd be able to hear me speaking to him, so I decided to give him a real pep talk that day. I'd also brought along his iPod, which previously had never been far away from him – it felt so wrong that he was in this remote place without any of his comforts.

I didn't really want to put anything right up to his ears, as there was still so much blood coming out of his brain and I couldn't imagine any sound being a good thing in his poor, damaged head. But music had always been so important to him, and the doctors had said it was worth a try. At the start of each day, my nerves would be raging as I worried about how Ally would be when we went in. Would he be in surgery again? Would he be in a bag? I found it hard even to walk through the door of the critical-care ward; Brenda and I would breathe deeply and compose ourselves, and then goad each other to open the door.

Once we were in, it was as if there was a big bass drum pulsing through my body as my eyes turned to Bed 4 in the corner – to see if he was alive, if he had a crowd of nurses around the bed, or if the dreaded curtains were drawn. But today we found him with a new male nurse, who was pushing his thumb hard into Ally's neck and shouting things like: 'Try to make me stop, Ally!' and 'Move my hand away, Ally!'

This was the day they would try to wake him up, as they had explained before, to see how much life was actually there. Every so often the nurses would come and try to provoke a reaction, shouting: 'Wake up, Ally!' and 'Who are you?' and 'What's your name?' It was awful to watch, and he just lay there, unresponsive. They would also conduct pain tests, cause him some minor pain to see if there was any reaction – which there wasn't.

When I arrived each morning I was desperate for an update, but the nurses were so busy and full-on that they couldn't spare the time to tell me what had happened, or what might happen next. There was never a dull moment: every 10 minutes there was a fussy little dance round the bed, as another liquid was shoved up a vein in his arm or groin. Brenda asked the nurse if he really had to be so brutal – it was clear that Ally was unable to move his hand away or do any of the other things they were asking of him. But Adrian said it had to be done: every tiny flicker was significant and needed to be recorded. But with Ally showing absolutely no responses so far, the nurses looked worried, and all we could do was look on in terror.

Suddenly, Ally began making a dreadful choking sound, and we watched as he turned all the colours of the rainbow, and the monitors went into a beeping frenzy. He was unconsciously rejecting his life-support tube. His nurse said they really needed to remove the tube, because he couldn't cope with it, but they couldn't take it out until he showed the smallest signs that he could breathe for himself.

That afternoon he was in an awful state, with lots of vomiting and choking. To clear his lungs, they had to put another tube right down his throat – so he now had two massive tubes going in, and his chest was producing a gurgling sound as loud as a car engine.

Watching it all, I found it impossible for a while to breathe properly myself. I didn't leave the bed for a moment that afternoon, not even to go to the loo or get something to eat or drink: I was working on pure adrenaline. I just stood on the floor of the ward, staring; I wasn't moving an inch.

We weren't allowed to sit around the bed at this stage, because the nurses had to be able to move quickly and freely around him. But from where I was I took a good long look at his face, noticing every pore of his skin; his eyelashes; his lips, which were cracked and covered with a white chalky substance; and his tongue, which was swollen and mauve and hanging out beside the life-support tube. His head was shaved in so many places now, and what hair he had was caked in dried blood. I'm usually such a squeamish person – I can't watch horror movies or stand the sight of blood, and I even pass out if I need to have an injection – and here I was, getting a full gory close-up of his head, which was like something out of Frankenstein. The drain for his brain fluid was held in place by a bolt and a spring-like thing embedded at the front of his skull, and his head looked dented underneath it. He had a bolt sticking out at the top, which was almost comedic, and near that were stitches and a lot of craters and shaved bits.

Dad and I agreed that Ally would find all of this fascinating, if only he could have seen it for himself. I was ushered outside the curtain when Ally started vomiting the horrible green stuff again, which they weren't happy with. But I was determined not to leave the room.

Looking around, I noticed for the first time a beautiful young Brazilian woman in the next bed: she was on life support and she hadn't woken either. What a cruel, cruel condition, I thought. She didn't have anyone around her yet, and I wondered what her story was.

I heard later that she was just 29 and she'd come to Britain for a new life, and she'd been working very hard, doing three jobs, so she could afford to bring her young daughter here from Brazil. Her husband had been worried about her blood pressure and how hard she was pushing herself and asked her to slow down, and then a week before her daughter was due to arrive, she'd suffered a massive stroke. Her husband and daughter came to sit with her, and I spoke to them and really hoped that things would get better for them soon as well.

You can see why so many TV dramas are set in hospitals: these places are always packed with emotional stories I knew that Ally really needed to breathe on his own and trigger the life support now, if he wasn't brain-dead.

I took out his iPod, and Brenda and I discussed at great length how close to his head the earpieces should go. After trying various arrangements, we settled for holding one earpiece each, about an inch away. I played him some songs he used to love: 'Brass Buttons' by Gram Parsons, and Emmylou Harris's version of Gram's song 'She'.

Hearing the intro to that song, I suddenly couldn't help myself and tears started streaming down my face. Up to this point, we'd ensured that nobody had cried around his bed – he would have said we were stupid to be all round him, weeping – but the sentiment of the song was unbearable.

He looked calm, even content in a way, for the first time since the seizure. He was stable on the life support, and for half an hour or so we just stared silently at him. Then there was the tiniest flicker of his eyelashes… and then another.

'Oh my God, did we actually see that?' we asked ourselves. 'Yes, we did!' His eyes didn't open, but it seemed a good sign.

Adrian came back to do more tests and observations: 'What's your name? Wake up, Ally! Tell me to stop! Stop the pain, Ally!'

The nurses marked down the eye flickers on a chart next to the bed, which up to now had read '0 0 0 0 0', zeroes in every column. There was a changeover of nurses at 8pm and

Brenda and I had to leave for a while, so we went to the hospital chapel and lit a candle, which I put in row three, three candles along. I didn't care if it was superstitious nonsense: I just had to increase Ally's chances in whatever way I could, and I knew that many Christians considered three a lucky number, because of the Holy Trinity. I talked to God for ages and ages.

I remembered reading that if you summon the archangels Raphael and Michael, you can sometimes see the sparkle of jade-green lights, and I scanned the dome of the chapel for signs of that colour until my neck ached.

When we went back into the ward to say good-night to Ally, the nurse pointed to the breathing monitor, and explained that when the green line started with a bit of red, it meant he was triggering the life support with a tiny bit of his own breath – and since we'd been gone she'd counted three breaths. Maybe the angels had come!

I jumped for joy and rushed into the waiting room to tell everyone the news, while the nurse looked on disapprovingly.

For us it was a great step forward, but they still weren't very satisfied with his progress, and they weren't offering a lot of hope. We were asked to leave to get some rest, and once again I was advised to be 'realistic', which seemed to be the watchword of the week. But it was impossible while everything continued to feel like a dream, and while I still felt emotionally numb.

At times I felt that what was happening wasn't my life at all, but a movie: I'd half-expect the director to yell 'Cut!' and Ally to immediately sit up and say 'Now get me away from this strip lighting and let's get some truffle pasta!' That's how realistic I was being.

On Day 3, I wrote in my diary:

Trying to wake him, they bully, poke, shout and stick things down his throat. We need to wake him to assess the neurological damage. He's sort of done a few eye flickers. They're dragging him back a bit.

He's vomited 5 times, it's green, they aren't happy. He really needs to breathe on his own to get the tube out.

I try him with a bit of Gram on the iPod. He does 3 breaths on his own and starts triggering the life support a bit.

Pray for breathing.

CHAPTER 6

As I tried to make sense of what was happening to us, I started to grade the days according to how things had gone and how I was feeling, giving them a rating from one star (truly awful) to five stars (amazing) in my diary.

Day 4 – Friday, September 11 – received just one star, because I felt deflated: the progress of Day 3 began to fade into the distance. Ally was still doing some breathing for himself and triggering his life support, but not enough and with very little strength. And he still couldn't cope with the life-support tube, which was why the surgeons had had a meeting that morning to discuss whether to take it out; but they decided it was too risky right now.

The senior nurse that day told me straight out that Ally wasn't going to make it, and the words of the surgeons on Day 1 came straight back to me: that 96% of grade-5 patients who don't die before they reach the hospital die within four days. The other 4% don't usually make it through the vasospasms that follow. (I've grown to dread that word, 'vasospasms'. I can barely type it now. I hear the word spoken in my head by the voice of Regan, the girl possessed by the Devil in The Exorcist.) I had been wishing so hard for Ally not to have vasospasms. I had pleaded with God in the hospital chapel – 'Please, please, don't let him get those' – and I'd been telling everyone that it wasn't his fate, that he definitely wouldn't have any. But secretly I had an awful feeling that he would, and that it was inevitable.

Ally was very poorly in the night, said the nurse, and he wasn't stabilizing. He advised us to stay here, close by him. Though the nurse didn't offer any hope, he did everything he could to comfort us; he saw that we were trying to keep our spirits up, and he joined in with our laughter when we joked that Ally's partly shaved hairstyle looked a bit like Phil Oakey's in the 1980s, when the Human League singer wore his hair long on one side and short on the other.

While the staff were doing everything in their power to keep Ally alive, and I loved and admired every single one of them, it annoyed me that they were talking about him so impersonally as if he was gone already, or would be in a matter of hours. I wanted to say 'That's my *husband* lying there!' They didn't know him; they hadn't seen him the week before, when he was making lovely home-made soup from the vegetables he grew in our garden, or when he was strolling around the National Portrait Gallery in London, talking about how he would put his own photographs on display if he had the space somewhere. I felt really sure that if they'd known him properly, they'd absolutely love him and think he was really special just like I did, but of course they could only see the patient he'd become, another critical case fighting for his life.

After I left the room, letting my dad and Brenda in to see Ally, I sat down in the waiting room and took my mobile phone out – the first time I'd done that since this had all happened. I'd given Ally's phone to Big Paul, because I hadn't been able to cope with speaking to anyone: there was absolutely nothing to say, at least until I knew if he was going to live or die. Over a cup of green tea made by my mum, I started reading all these lovely text messages from my friends and colleagues, sending me and Ally their prayers and best wishes. But I was in no emotional condition to answer any of them yet.

Mum couldn't bring herself to go in and see Ally, and I couldn't blame her: he was in an awful state and there was no recognizable 'Ally' there. So she stayed in the waiting room, along with Alistair, Paul, Sandra and Steve, to lend support whenever we were ushered out of the ward. I told Mum it was a shame that the nurses didn't know who Ally really was as a person, and she came up with a great idea.

She suggested that she photocopy lots of pictures of him that evening, which I could stick all round his bed so when new nurses took over, they'd see he was a talented young man with a hell of a lot to live for. And I wanted them to see how handsome he was, as well.

Going through all the text messages I'd received, I saw one from Pauline, the wife of Texas' manager, Rab Andrew. Her text told me to go and ask for the archangels Michael, Raphael and Gabriel to go and sit with Ally – she said it was time for the big guns to intervene. It also gave me the names of some healing crystals to put by Ally's bed. I'd only met her once, at our wedding, but I felt compelled to reply to her text, although I hadn't even replied to any of my close friends, even my best female friend, Holly, at this stage.

It felt odd confiding in a near-stranger like this, but here I was, writing a long text to Pauline about Ally's condition and what needed to happen. I had this feeling that she could really help in some way. I told Pauline how important it was that Ally breathes on his own, and she replied that she would constantly visualize him breathing without any tube, and she would ask her friends who are healers to do the same.

This sounded exciting. I'd experimented with meditation in the past, and visualization is something I might have done inadvertently when I wished really hard for something. Believers in visualization say that by repeatedly focusing on certain images and ideas, you can actually bring about positive changes in the physical world. Apparently, all kinds of people these days, from Eastern yogis to stressed-out businesspeople, use visualization techniques to heal sickness, treat depression, correct bad habits, change their careers and improve their lives.

I told Dad what Pauline had written and he was so positive, saying we can go and buy the crystals and we would make it work. But I saw how exhausted this crisis had made him, and realized that he may have been even more scared than me. I knew Mum and Dad loved Ally and me unconditionally and always wanted our lives to be perfect, and we felt the same about them, and I was so sad for Mum and Dad that this was happening.

Dad and I decided to try some visualization for ourselves. We went into the chapel, sat down and started concentrating really hard. I pictured Ally with a massive pair of lungs, which were taking in deep breaths and letting them out effortlessly. The rest of his body looked like an anatomical diagram, with all the organs named, and as the air went into and out of his body, the organs started shifting into place and doing their thing. His heart became big and red and started making a lovely beating sound, and a big smile appeared on his face. All that concentration was so exhausting, our faces turned red.

I fell asleep for about 10 minutes in the warmth of that chapel, dribbling down my top, but Dad didn't wake me up. When I opened my eyes, I saw him staring into the dome.

I received another text from Pauline, saying that her friend Mishka had asked all the members of her healing circle to join in and help Ally. She said that if I texted her every night with details of what was needed and what they should concentrate on, they'd join forces and focus on that. I was stunned by the fact that strangers would be so kind.

Eventually I felt I had to go back to the ward, so I went to relieve Alistair, taking up my normal position standing to Ally's left. The staff were still trying desperately to wake him, with continual poking and shouting.

Around 3pm, a female nurse came and shouted at Ally to 'poke out your tongue... try really hard to poke it out', and as we watched with anticipation, suddenly his tongue came out. It was such a small thing, but he seemed to do it on command.

So, I asked myself, does that mean he can hear us? And he can understand words?

When the surgeons appeared around the bed that afternoon, I launched into a speech about how fabulous it was that he could understand words, and how all the choking and body movements meant he wasn't paralyzed. But they looked sorry for me, and explained that all the movements were simply reflexes and I didn't understand how poorly he really was.

But again I refused to be realistic – I was almost bouncing, I felt so positive – and I found myself saying 'Well, gentlemen, I'm delighted!' It sounded like something out of a comedy sketch, and Brenda and I actually fell about laughing after they left.

I decided I didn't care if the staff here thought I was an idiot. After all, despite centuries of scientific study of the human brain, there still seemed to be no rhyme or reason to things. Their answer to so many questions was 'We can't say' or 'There's no way of knowing' – so surely there was also no way of knowing whether I was right in thinking that Ally was going to come through this.

Brenda and I held Ally's hands through all the arterial lines going into his body (I was learning some of the medical lingo by now), but his senior nurse said we should be careful not to rub or stroke his skin, as it would be so sensitive that it would feel like fire or sandpaper to him. At one point, Brenda was sure that she'd felt his little finger squeeze her hand a little, as if he knew she was there. We both studied his little finger after that and urged him to repeat the trick – 'Do it again, Ally, we know you did it, go on' – but it didn't happen again.

For a long time, the nurses had been wanting to see him bite down on the life-support tube, which was the first sign of life they'd expect to see. And that day we saw his lips move – he was girning with his mouth – and the senior nurse confirmed he'd bitten down on the tube, and made a note of it. These tiny movements would normally be barely noticeable, but the significance of any movement was hugely magnified now. Whether Ally could hear us or not, we talked constantly to him, telling him where he was and discussing stories from the day's newspapers. When I was alone with him, I remembered that article about Richard Hammond and told him: 'If there's an easy road, don't you dare bloody take it!' I had a laugh with him about it, as he'd have expected me to – 'Don't make me come in there and get you out!' I joked. That was when his mouth moved ever so slightly upwards at the sides. He smiled! Well, as far as I was concerned, it was definitely a smile.

My heart skipped and I ran into the waiting room to tell everyone. Everyone who knew Ally well would have understood how important that smile was. He'd always been daft and cheeky, with a terrific sense of humour, and before this had happened he'd been able to make me laugh every day of our lives. One of our favourite games was to mess around with famous song lyrics, changing the ubiquitous word 'love' to 'glove' – 'The Greatest Glove Of All', 'Glove Will Tear Us Apart', and 'Love To Glove You, Baby'. It sounds childish, but it was guaranteed to have both of us roaring with laughter.

He didn't swear a lot but he'd been brilliant at putting swearwords in songs as well. We'd once sat in the bath together and rewritten the whole of Bob Dylan's Blood On The Tracks album with well-placed rude words like bum, fart and tit! Ally had given us the biggest laugh ever on our holiday at Maggie and Janey's place in Umbria.

We'd all gone to bed one night, but it was still 30C outside and Janie had got up to lie on the sofa next to the open window in the lounge to cool off. Meanwhile, Ally had got up to the loo in the darkness, and after that he'd stood at the window in just his underpants, totally unaware that Janey was there. After about 10 minutes he suddenly realized he was standing right next to Janey's head.

Janey is very proper and she'd tried to lie there as still as possible rather than say anything and embarrass him, but when she saw he'd noticed her she leapt up and said 'Cup of tea?' When they told us the story, Maggie and I were in fits.

'Oh my God, what if you'd sat down?' Maggie said. 'I'd have got my bags and gone home!' Ally replied. After the incident,

Ally loved to make us laugh by telling Janey: 'I'll see you at the window in my pants at 2!'

So Ally's smile was great news – for a while. When people tell you that a serious health crisis like this is 'all ups and downs', they're not kidding. Before we had to leave for the nurse changeover at 10pm that day, not only had Ally stopped giving any responses, but his heart rate and blood pressure had gone through the roof again. His temperature had also reached 41, indicating another infection, which they couldn't identify. But they told us they'd try another course of antibiotics, and give him a lumbar puncture in the night to see if that would give them some answers. I felt his life really was in the balance that night, that he might be going now, and I really didn't want to leave him. If he was about to die, I had to be there.

When I got in Dad's car to go home, I did a ridiculous thing: I actually took out my mobile and called Ally's phone to give him the latest news. I was all ready to say: 'Oh my gawd, you'll never believe what happened...' It was pure reflex. I missed him so much, and it was exactly what I would have done in normal life, if Ally hadn't been lying there in the hospital.

The nights had settled into a routine. After we returned home from the hospital, Brenda, Alistair and I would wave my mum and dad off, then sit in the kitchen to discuss the day's events. We'd do it for hours, mulling everything over. I would be really positive, and when I couldn't do that any more,

Brenda would take up the baton, and we handed it back and forth that way for as long as we could. I really lost it that night when I got into the bath.

When I was lying back, I just happened to notice some patches of wall under the windowsill that Ally had missed when he'd been painting the bathroom, and I couldn't bear it any longer. I put my head under the water and primal-screamed, but with no sound, because Alistair and Brenda were in the bedroom next door and I didn't want them waking up in another panic. We'd all been putting on a brave face for such a long time. It was like being on a war march – 'Come on, everybody, stiff upper lip! We're going in and getting him out! We can do this, people!' But suddenly it all seemed so helpless to me. Even in my best-case scenario, if he survived these next few days, he would be a vegetable, both physically and mentally, who most probably wouldn't know who the hell I was. I tried to get that image out of my head, thinking that it would come true if I pictured it happening, and I just couldn't let that be the case.

I was screaming silently to God, pleading with him not to let that happen. No matter what I did, I couldn't get the idea of the horrible vasospasms out of my mind. Go away! Go away! But they wouldn't go away.

I held my breath underwater and screamed soundlessly for what felt like five minutes, with my face contorted and frozen in terror. And then something extraordinary happened. A sudden peace, a massive calm, came over me. My face immediately relaxed and I stopped crying, and I dried myself and went to the window, smiled and said 'Thank you.' Whatever had come to me made no noise, and came as a feeling rather than using any words. Although I'm an open-minded, spiritual person, I've always had a problem with blind faith: I always thought it was amazing, and I'd love to be able to live like that, but I really need things to be proven to me.

Something profound seemed to happen in the bath that night, though. I didn't tell anyone at the time, for fear of people thinking I'd completely lost it at this desperate time. And you know what? Maybe I did!

My diary entry for Day 4 ends:

This arvo he pokes out his tongue on command. This is good. He also tries to squeeze his mum's finger. He is girning and grimacing, and he does a big bite down on the tube, and he smiles.

I think he's there!!

CHAPTER 7

Every day, I had a permanent knot in my belly that I could feel even when I was asleep. And when I woke, an overpowering feeling of dread and doom hit me as soon as my eyes opened. So this is what sheer terror feels like, I remember thinking.

When I went back in to see Ally on Day 5, the breathing tube had gone. It had gone! He had a mask on, and two little tubes up his nose, but his mouth was free now. His lips were slightly parted, and I could see how cracked and sore they were. He had started to breathe for himself during the night, so he had been taken to surgery and had the tube removed.

It was great news, though at this stage every step forward seemed to be followed by several steps back, and his life was still hanging in the balance. But I was so happy, my heart felt as if it was jumping out of my chest.

The medical bullying began early that day; every 20 minutes it was: 'Poke your tongue out!' or 'Open your eyes!' or 'Squeeze my hand, Ally!' or 'Your wife is here! Open your eyes and say hello, Ally!' They still had no idea how much neurological damage had been done, but they expected that because of the bleeding all over his brain, he'd have aphasia, which is an inability to find words and communicate.

They said there was a huge risk that he would have an 'infarct', which is an area of dead brain tissue. This news should have made me weep like a widow over his bed, but instead I started giggling because it sounded like 'fart'. I laughed like a naughty child, and I knew that Ally would have as well. Laughter seemed really inappropriate amid all the tragedy, but maybe it was an unconscious strategy to reduce the stress and keep myself sane. And I wasn't the only one.

Dad was with me, and I said to him 'Fancy calling something like that an infarct!' And we both fell about. One of the staff explained that the dead tissue doesn't regenerate, but that over time the brain can find new ways to do things. What did 'over time' mean, I asked. 'A long time,' he replied. What, about five years? 'No – decades.' Bugger!

He listed the functions and skills that were likely to be seriously affected by the damage to different parts of Ally's brain – including his motor skills, speech, behaviour, memory, movement, and control of his body temperature and blood pressure. I hadn't even considered that he might lose his ability to swallow. I had to face the fact that he might never be able to eat without a tube, never lift his hand to throw a ball, never sit up straight, and never know when he needs to go to the loo – all of the everyday things we normally take for granted. I couldn't believe it. Imagine having to learn every single ability all over again – even how to hold your head up, the way a baby does. The brain can rewire itself, but it takes a long time, the consultant explained.

'There is no short-term solution to neurological damage, Mrs McErlaine. Please start to consider what we are telling you.' That's when I asked myself: if he lives, can I look after him? Can I be his carer? And I decided I had to: if that's what I had to do, that's what I'd do and we'd get through it. Well, I would get through it by myself – Ally wouldn't be with me, not really. And that struck me as the saddest and loneliest thing ever: he'd be a constant reminder of the man I missed and desperately wanted back.

The machines all around Ally gleamed in the sunlight coming through the window, and as Ally lay there, Dad told him he looked like he was in a massive spacecraft, and he'd find it all very interesting when he woke up. And Ally suddenly lifted an eyebrow as if to say: 'Oh, really?'

I just saw your eyebrow move, Ally,' said Dad. 'I know you can hear us now.' And Ally flickered an eyelash ever so slightly.

That morning, we stuck up a lot of pictures of Ally around the bed with Blu-Tack, as we'd decided the day before – loads of shots of him laughing, having fun and being daft. Some from our wedding day, some from our recent holiday in Italy, a shot of his beloved Alfa Romeo 147 Collezione car, and some photographs of his nieces and nephews. We covered the whole area around Bed 4 with brightly covered proof of his reasons for being on Earth. At first, the nurse on duty didn't seem to like it, but then she took a closer look and said she recognized him.

'He's the guitarist in the band Texas,' Dad explained.

'Oh!' she said. 'I love that band.'

Ally's medical doctor came to tell us that the latest lab results. They could hear how bad his chest infection was, but they still couldn't pinpoint what it was, so they were going to switch to another course of antibiotics. They couldn't do that straight away, because Ally was being pumped with so many different things and everything had to be carefully balanced, and ordering the drugs was quite a long-winded procedure.

I asked if they could speed it up a bit, as his temperature had gone right up to 40C, but the doctor smiled and said no, sorry. Because of his temperature, they put an inflatable ice-cold blanket over him. There was a constant hum around him now and we couldn't touch him. He was boiling up, his heart rate was still so high that there was the risk of cardiac arrest, and his machines were going mental. But although he wasn't stabilizing, they were still relentlessly trying to wake him up:

the only way they could find the extent of the neurological damage was to see what movements he could make on command, and whether he could feel pain.

At one point, when Sandra and I were yakking away to him, he made what looked like a small yawn, and we laughed so hysterically that we were told to be quiet. Sandra and I talked and laughed there for a good hour, managing to bring a lighter mood to the clinical and frightening environment of this hospital ward. Ally made a few eyelash flickers, and it seemed as if he was there with us.

In the past, there'd been a running joke between us all about Ally's height. Sandra is taller than him, at 5ft 11in, and Ally had always claimed to be 5ft 10in when he was really 5ft 9in. Now Sandra was teasing him.

'It's weird how short you look lying down, Ally,' she said.

He gave a tiny smile as if he was hearing every word. I absolutely knew Ally was in there now. I didn't know how much of him remained, but I was sure he was making these tiny movements as a direct response to what we were saying. And every time we saw a flicker, one of us would run into the waiting room and share it with the others.

Despite all those movements, only that single poke of the tongue had been recorded on his chart as an action made on command. By this point, I was so detached from ordinary life that I didn't give a shit about music, or if I ever made any again. I never thought I'd ever say that: music had been my life. That day, I thought about our fellow Red Sky July member Charity and how her world had suddenly fallen away.

One minute it was all go – the album was going to be made, the money was in, everyone was totally in love with the music, we should have been in rehearsals and we were due to start recording in two weeks – and the next minute there was nothing. She hadn't taken Ally's situation well – she loved him and was so scared – but I couldn't let her see him yet: he was too poorly and he wouldn't have wanted it. But I couldn't leave Ally's bedside, not even for a toilet break, unless they made me. I was a physical mess at this point: I hadn't eaten a morsel for five days, and I'd thrown up nearly every morning before we'd left for the hospital. The situation had completely robbed me of my appetite and all interest in food, so eating a meal became an unpleasant and pointless thing to do. I seemed to be surviving on green tea, and maybe the odd nut or piece of banana, and I was seriously losing weight.

At the time, there was a panic about swine flu. That was a big worry because if any of us got it we wouldn't be allowed into the ward, and I felt Ally would die without us there. So I was putting so much of the antibacterial cleaner on my hands, the tops of my fingers had split.

Eventually, Sandra and I returned to the waiting room so Big Paul and Dave could go in to see Ally. Big Paul, who's really called Paul Maxwell, is 6ft 4in and has a fantastically loud Belfast-accented voice. He used to be in a punk band called Protex, and Ally and Paul shared a love of many things, including music and golf. Paul and Dave did a lot of talking to Ally, to see if they could stimulate a reaction.

Suddenly, Paul and Dave ran back into the waiting room, causing me to jump up, thinking something was terribly wrong.

In fact, they were excited about what had just happened. Debbie the nurse had shouted: 'Ally, who's this?' and Ally had said the words: 'Paul Maxwell'.

I made Paul tell me the story six or seven times, asking him what Ally's voice had sounded like. He said it was a whisper, and slightly robotic, but that there was absolutely no doubt he'd said it. Dave laughed, and said how worried they'd been about breaking the news that my husband's first words were 'Paul Maxwell', instead of my own name. I'd only been shouting: 'What's my name, babe?' to him for 48 hours!

But I thought it was wonderful and danced for joy. It told me that not only did he have the ability to recognize people, so he had his memory, but that he could form words and speak as well. We'd got to know a lady in the waiting room quite well; her name was Lesley and her son was in medical intensive care.

Now Lesley gave me a hug, but as she did so she whispered in my ear: 'Remember, it's one step forward and 10 back…'

Full of hope now, I returned to Ally and stood over him, but there were no more responses from him. They told me that what he'd done would have been like moving a mountain, and he'd be tired out now.

As the cooling blanket hummed away, I blew cool air onto his forehead. Then I took out my diary and told him I was giving the day four stars. And I leant towards his ear, very close to the brain drain, and told him 'I can look after you – I know I can. We won't need help.'

When I left the hospital that night, I was elated, petrified and exhausted all at the same time. 'I can sense him, I think,' I wrote in my diary, 'but he's so far away.'

CHAPTER 8

ALLY always loved Camden, especially the little kebab house called Marathon opposite Chalk Farm tube station. Now I was travelling through Camden in the back of Karen and Dave's car, en route to the hospital for my daily visit.

We reached a familiar zebra crossing and had to stop; I counted the seconds for a while, until we were able to move again. This time last week, Ally and I had walked across that zebra crossing. I remembered what a gorgeous sunny day it had been, and how we'd still been tanned from our holidays. We'd come to Camden to check out the vintage-clothing shops and to have some freshly squeezed orange juice from the bloke on the corner, as we often did at the weekend in the summer.

Now, on this Sunday morning a week later, I watched a couple holding hands, all dressed up for a promenade around Stables Market. That was us last week – that was what we'd been doing. And I was struck by how most other people's lives were continuing as normal, while ours were frozen in time.

There was a building to my left that I always used to point out to Ally. It was where Prince used to have his own shop, and Mum used to take me there when I was young. I'd swear I was going to make loads of money out of music so I could buy a ticket to Minneapolis and marry him (because obviously he'd fall in love with me instantly).

When I was 15 I read that he only liked ladies with dark hair, so I dyed my mousy hair raven black. A year earlier I'd had a perm, trying to look like Susanna Hoffs of The Bangles, but unfortunately there was nothing you could do to change the face back then!

When I got to the hospital that morning, Ally's eyes were slightly open. But they were gazing straight ahead, not tracking anything and devoid of emotion. The nurse told me that during the latest observations they'd asked him what his wife's name was, and he'd said: 'Shelly McErlaine'.

That felt so great: he knew me, and knew we were married. I had to leave when they came in to clean him up a bit, and I went straight down to the hospital chapel, lit the third candle in the third row, and said a massive thank-you to God, Jesus and all the angels. But the knot in my stomach felt like it was getting bigger, and I didn't know why.

That day, I started sending out a round-robin text message to friends to keep them updated. I also asked Karen to go on Facebook and post an update, because Ally's page and my page were inundated with wonderful messages and lots of questions. I heard that a Scottish newspaper had published a story about Ally, but they'd got the date of the seizure wrong, and I felt it was important to keep the people who loved him properly informed.

Ally couldn't move the fluids in his body himself, so every four hours they turned his body, propping him up with pillows. They'd ask me to leave for that, so every time that happened I went into the waiting room to write the round-robin text. I'd send it to a dozen people, and each of those people would forward it to another set of people, and so on. I found out later that there was a network of about 1,000 people getting these texts. The more the better – all those thoughts and prayers and all that goodwill had to count for something. Ally was still under the cooling blanket, running a high temperature, and the nurses had a lot of sweat to mop up. There were lots of long beeps and flatlines, but nothing too serious.

He did a few eyebrow lifts (they might have just been spasms, but I was calling them eyebrow lifts), and I was sure he knew I was there. He still needed all his energies to fight the awful infections and the swelling of his brain, so I didn't want a lot of people coming in. But I'd agreed that his cousin Gerald could come today. Ally kept his eyes shut most of the time, but I think he liked Gerald coming: when the nurse asked: 'Who's this?', Ally said: 'Gerald' and smiled. Then he seemed to drift off again, and I wondered if he could still hear us in this other place he kept returning to.

I wanted to know what he was feeling, and the doctors told me he would be numb in a lot of places, but his skin would have a burning sensation. They said his head might feel as if he had a terrible hangover – only his consciousness wouldn't know anything about it, which sounded very odd. It was almost a relief that he was comatose: I couldn't bear the idea of him being in pain or confused whenever he surfaced and responded to us.

The helplessness I felt was awful. Like my dad, I'd usually been able to sort things out in my life, and could do most things I put my mind to. But it really hurt that I couldn't do anything about Ally. Or maybe I could... Pauline had sent some crystals in the post, and I needed to get home and look at them soon, find out what they were all for. That night he had a lovely male nurse from New Zealand, and I asked him if he could go easy on Ally during the observations. I'd been seeing signs in Ally's face that he could feel pain but that he couldn't do anything about it.

He asked if I'd actually seen his face move in response to pain. I replied that I hadn't, but that I could tell when he felt pain: somehow his face took on a darker look. I said I felt he was constantly waiting for me, as his wife, to jump in and say: 'Whoa there a minute, mister! What the fuck do you think you're doing? He's telling you to get off, in his own way!' The nurse laughed – he had a great sense of humour, and although I absolutely hated leaving Ally again, I was pleased he'd be with him for the few hours I'd be asleep.

I said goodbye, and Ally lifted his left forearm as if to wave. It was such a small gesture, but it definitely happened. I decided that day, Sunday, September 13, was a good day, and I gave it five stars in my little red Smythson diary, which before this tragedy had been used just for future work dates and social events.

Darkness… I realized that the house was in total darkness. I'd woken up with a start and almost didn't know where I was. 'Ally's not here,' I thought. No, of course he wasn't there. The phone was ringing. Oh my God, the phone!

I ran around naked, repeating 'Oh my God, oh my God, oh my God!' in a high-pitched voice. I knew where the phone was: it was in its holder in the kitchen, where I'd vowed to keep it ever since I wasted precious seconds looking for it on that awful morning when they took Ally away in an ambulance.

'Hello?' says a voice from the phone. 'It's the National Hospital in Queen Square. Is that Mrs McErlaine? Can you come in, please? He's taken a turn...'

It felt as if my heart actually stopped then, and I was suspended in time. I knew I ought to run and get dressed, but everything seemed to be in slow motion. Alistair and Brenda were up, and we phoned Dave. I didn't know if it was still night or the next morning, but it was 5am. Dave arrived around an hour later to pick us up, and we headed for the hospital.

It would have been easier to take the lift to the first floor, where Ally was, but I never took it because on the first day here, Dad and I had seen a guy in a Celtic shirt waiting on the stairs. Because Ally was a huge Celtic fan, we decided they might be lucky. So I ran up the stairs with Brenda.

On Sunday night, all of Ally's responses had stopped. Around 2am they'd taken him for a brain scan, and there were no signs of life and no movement – apart from the fact that the vasospasms had started. It was horrible news. Mum, Dad, Paul and Sandra arrived around 9am. But there was so much going on in the ward, none of us were allowed to see him, and we had to play the waiting game again.

There was a terrible sadness in that waiting room: the mood had changed completely, it was the lowest any of us had been so far, and everybody was crying. I kept looking for someone important to talk to, but I couldn't find anyone. I was desperate to see him and let him know I was here, but the curtains were drawn around his bed the whole time.

We stood there for ages with our faces pressed against the tiny viewing window, waiting for a sign – any sign at all. Could nobody tell us **anything**? Then I saw Dr Silverhair rushing out of the ward.

'I need to speak to you urgently,' he told me, and at that moment I thought I'd lost the power to breathe.

We were locked in the waiting room again, this time with the doctor, two surgeons and a nurse. The atmosphere was very sombre, and for a long time nobody seemed to want to break the silence. Then the doctor addressed us, though he seemed unable to look me in the face.

'I'm afraid Ally has vasospasms,' he said. 'We believe they are severe. Also, the scan that we did last night has come back, and I'm very sorry to tell you Ally has two frontal-lobe strokes. We're not sure if they're due to the initial bleed or the onset of the spasms.'

Oh, my God, no – frontal-lobe strokes had been my biggest fear. I remembered seeing some dreadful horror film in which someone had a frontal lobotomy, and then it was knickers off, knobs out, and everyone dancing around with sexual abandon and absolutely no regard for the consequences.

I had so many questions. If the strokes were the result of the initial bleed, wouldn't they have shown up in the scans he'd had before?

'No,' he replied, 'they take up to four days sometimes to show up.' But Ally was responding with words yesterday, and he knew who everybody was – so if he already had the strokes then, didn't that mean he still had those abilities?

'We can't say. The spasms change a lot of things.' He said they didn't know exactly why the vasospasms start: you just get them with severe subarachnoid haemorrhages. Oh great, I thought – working in the dark again. But he described how they would try to keep him alive throughout the vasospasms.

The spasms would stop the brain from receiving oxygen, which meant he could just shut down completely at any second. So they'd keep him in a highly hypertensive state, with his blood pressure ramped up to the maximum, so that as much oxygenated blood as possible could get to his brain. It was very dangerous, the chances of another stroke were very high, but it was the only thing they could do.

Sometimes they could put a special tube known as a stent in a patient's artery, but they weren't sure if that was a good idea for Ally – they were going to look into that. We could all see the scan if we wanted to – take a look at the frontal-lobe strokes – and everyone followed the doctor to do that, except me. I didn't want to; I felt completely and utterly destroyed already, and seeing the evidence would only have made me feel worse, if that was possible. Basically, Ally was fucked, I was fucked, it was all fucked.

Every now and then, I heard a powerful voice inside my head that completely disagreed with that verdict. It was saying 'This is **not** his lot! This isn't!' Sometimes I heard the words spoken by my own voice, but at other times it was a male voice, and I wondered if it was Ally communicating with me.

Oh, great – so now I was hearing voices! When the others came back, they told me how tiny the strokes looked on the scan. Dad said they were like two grey hairline cracks.

They were almost not there at all – but then we didn't know what they were supposed to look like; maybe everyone's strokes looked tiny. I gave a bit of a speech then to the staff, telling them they didn't know Ally, and he wouldn't be hanging on in there if he wasn't ready for a big old fight.

We aren't worried, I said, because we're all sure that he's coming back, and that he'll be back to normal again; we aren't giving up, so please don't **you** give up! They raced off to get Ally ready for the treatment to counter the vasospasms, and I had the feeling I deserved an Oscar for Best Actress. When we finally got to see Ally around 9pm, he looked as if there was nothing there, no personality – he'd gone. His blood pressure had been pushed up so high he'd turned mauve. He was shaking violently, and I tried in vain to hold his legs down.

It all felt so hopeless – he was dying – and I had to go and sit down. Dave went in to see him on his own, and in desperation he tried a new strategy, going right up to his face and giving him a good talking to.

'I know you're in there, Ally,' he said. 'You know you've got to fight now more than ever. Shelly needs you now, Al. Step up to it, mate. You know how important it is that you fight hard, don't you? Don't you?'

And Ally whispered one word: 'Yes.'

He was alive!

CHAPTER 9

It was now Tuesday, September 15 – a week since the seizure, and looking back, it felt like a lifetime. When I went into the kitchen that morning, I noticed a huge pile of letters, and I felt that I should open them – see what's happening in the real world – but I still couldn't face that. Then I spotted a letter that didn't look as scary as the others. I opened it, and found it was from Rab's wife, Pauline. I'd received some more text messages from her, but with so much going on at the hospital over the past few days, I hadn't had time to reply.

The letter explained that Pauline's friend Mishka had a healing circle of about 30 people in Glasgow, and that they'd be visualizing and group-healing for Ally; they'd also do some extra healing for me. She asked me to tell them if there was anything in particular that Ally needed, and they would work on specific things. How amazing, I thought, that strangers would do this for me. She'd enclosed some more crystals, and said I should put them by his bed if I could. I held these beautiful stones in my hand; they were as cold as ice, but felt amazing. I was inspired to do some research online about crystals, and I read that they are used extensively in alternative medicine; because of their very special structure, it's believed that crystals respond to a wide range of energies, and their rates of vibration have the power of changing people's auras and healing both the body and the mind.

I used to carry some 'lucky stones' when I was in Alisha's Attic. I had a tiny pouch of lucky things that I took everywhere with me, including crystals and Guatemalan 'worry dolls'. Though I'd decided the crystals were lucky, I saw them as just pretty, shiny, inert objects that felt nice to hold; I didn't know they could actually be useful and powerful. But holding a piece of smoky quartz in my hand now, I had the very strong sense that it wasn't lifeless. I decided to take it in that day and put it under Ally's pillow.

I also printed out some of the information about crystals I'd found, so I could read it out to Ally – when nobody else was listening, so they didn't think I'd gone mental. I wasn't sure he'd understand it in his condition, but he'd have to listen at least!

There was nothing on Ally's charts that morning – indicating that he wasn't responding in any way – and the staff were very concerned. The vasospasms were continuing, so his life seemed to be hanging by a thread. But his 'yes' to Dave the night before had given us hope; we didn't believe that he was as badly affected by the strokes as they did. His temperature was still worryingly high, but I'd brought him some flannels to keep him cool: white and green – Celtic colours! He'd been tidied up a bit – he'd had the staples taken out of his head, and the hair that remained on his head had been brushed, so he looked a lot more like my Ally.

I sang to him – 'Jolene' by Dolly Parton, 'She' by Gram Parsons, and even 'My Favourite Things' in my best Julie Andrews voice. That'll tickle him, I thought – and sure enough, he gave me a definite look, so I was sure he could hear me. But he spent most of the time asleep, looking calm and smiling quite a lot.

The next morning, he looked quite aware for a full minute: he smiled again, and when I asked if he wanted Alistair and Dave to come in, he nodded. His temperature had come down to 38, which was a good sign. He wasn't speaking initially, but we heard that last night he'd spoken his date of birth, October 31, 1968. That was amazing – despite the damned strokes and the vasospasms, he knew who he was.

Then came another small breakthrough: Brenda said hello to him, and he replied 'Hello, Mum.' But after that, the silence descended again for a long time. The staff had a big meeting about Ally today, because they had a dilemma. There was a whirring sound in his chest, which they thought was fluid on the lungs, and he had a massive open bedsore on the back of one of his legs – so although he was having vasospasms and they were concerned about moving him, they thought they really ought to change his position and shift his fluids. The bedsore was a worry, because he didn't need any more infections – he already had countless tubes going into his body, and there literally wasn't a single spare vein left for any more intravenous medication.

So they lifted him, using a big blue hoist attached to a pulley on the ceiling. They had to carry him right up into the air to put him on a gigantic wheeled chair, so he was sitting up. It was one of the saddest sights I'd ever seen, poor Ally being pulled about like this without him knowing. I was glad he wasn't aware of what was happening: if he had, he would've shat himself. His head was supported with a brace, and his torso was strapped in as well. And his legs were sticking out – the first time I'd seen his legs since he'd come here. They were thin like you wouldn't believe.

Where had he gone, I wondered – I'd had no idea that muscles could waste so quickly. He was been dressed in a hospital gown, with an old-lady white blanket over him, and he just stared ahead blankly, not tracking anything. Back when they started trying to wake him up, they told us that if he had his eyes open, we should try to engage him in conversation, because he might spontaneously respond.

I sat down in a seat next to his big chair, and said: 'Blimey, Ally, that must have felt weird being moved like that.'

'Yep, it did, actually,' he replied, making me jump out of my skin. I didn't recognize his voice – it was higher than normal, and sounded robotic.

'Oh my God!' I said, 'did you just speak?'

But he went blank again – it was so frustrating that he kept doing this, coming back for a moment and then suddenly leaving again. A moment later I noticed his eyes were open again, though they still weren't tracking anything. And then he said: 'There's something on her dress.' What dress? I was wearing a rollneck and jeans, and there was nobody there wearing a dress. I asked what dress he could see, and he looked very confused.

Ally's speech therapist had said he almost definitely had aphasia – language impairment – but I didn't believe that. It can be partial, though – some people with aphasia can speak but can't write, and some can't speak though they can sing, which sounds very strange; it depends on the area of the brain that's damaged, and the extent of the damage. The therapist said she had to wait until he was more responsive to test him properly, but I suspected aphasia was off the menu: although what he'd said didn't seem to relate to anything, they were real words, in a real sentence, weren't they? He definitely had dysphagia, the inability to swallow. He was given some apple syrup today to see if he could swallow that, and he coughed and almost choked and threw it up over me and Brenda. And the dysphagia was down to brain damage: his brain had basically forgotten how to do it. Considering how much Ally loved his food, I found it incredible that his brain had forgotten how to swallow.

They were still pushing his blood pressure up through the roof to protect him against the vasospasms, and after he'd been in the chair for about half an hour, the machines started bleeping, he started panicking and turned a bright purple colour. They hoisted him up really quickly and put him back into bed. The doctors said it would have been agony for him to sit up for a long time, as his muscles were in such bad condition, but he'd have to learn to do it in stages, and they were very pleased he'd managed it for half an hour. When he was all unstrapped and lying down again, I got my piece of smoky quartz out and slipped it under his pillow. A nurse saw me and disapproved, saying it wasn't advisable to bring things in, but I chose not to listen. I'd already put something else under the pillow, anyway. The previous evening, our very dear friends Connor and Louisa had come to the hospital, and Louisa had pressed a crucifix into my hand, saying it was a cross from Italy that had been blessed by Padre Pio, and she believed it had healed her friend's little girl.

Padre Pio was a famous saint – he was the highly venerated Italian priest who was reputed to have the stigmata of Christ appear regularly on his body. So I'd taken the cross to the hospital chapel and told the little ceramic figure of Jesus there: 'I'm putting this under his pillow. Please make it work.'

I'd given the other nurses strict instructions not to move it whenever they changed Ally's bed or turned his body, and I'd constantly checked to make sure it was still there. Now it was joined under the pillow by a crystal – which I figured God had made anyway, so it was all his work under there.

Big Paul came in that day with a letter Ally had received from our good friend Dougie Souness. Ally had known Dougie since he was a kid; when Ally was 12 and had started to play the guitar, he used to hang out with Dougie and his friend Bill. Ally looked up to them: they were a few years older, played drums and guitar and loved rock music.

When Ally was 15 he got an evening job stacking shelves in a supermarket; he earned £16 a week, most of which he'd spend on records and guitar strings. One day in the early 1980s, he treated himself to a limited-edition Space Shuttle-shaped vinyl picture disc of the Rush single 'Countdown', and on the way home he spotted Dougie and Bill and waved the record proudly at them: 'Look what I've got!'

Dougie behaved like a bit of a hardnut in those days, and would take the piss out of Ally for liking Rush, who Dougie thought were crap. So Dougie did something impulsive then, just for a laugh. He casually walked up to Ally, grabbed the record and, without saying a word, smashed it to pieces and walked on. Ally was devastated. Dougie being the lovely bloke he really is, he went straight to the record shop and tried to get Ally a replacement. He couldn't get the picture disc, so he got him a Uriah Heep single instead, and refunded the cost of the Rush single as well. Ally used the money to buy a replacement 'Countdown' picture disc.

Years later, Dougie went on to manage Wet Wet Wet and several other Scottish bands, and in 2008 he was backstage at a Rush gig, so he told the story to the band. He got the whole band to sign a poster for Ally, which reads 'I hope this draws a line under this sorry episode', and that had become Ally's latest pride and joy.

So here was a letter from Dougie, which Big Paul had been nominated to read because of his big, clear voice. The letter gave Ally some news about his friends and Glasgow, and ended with the interesting lines:

'Invisible airways crackle with life

Bright antennae bristle with the energy

Emotional feedback on timeless wavelength

Bearing a gift beyond price, almost free.'

'That's lovely,' I said to Paul. 'What is it?'

Paul said it wasn't like Dougie to write a poem. Maybe it was a lyric to a song? Maybe it's a song Ally likes... And Ally, comatose under his cool blanket, having failed for four hours to move or respond to anything, suddenly whispered one word: 'Rush.'

The words were from the song 'The Spirit of Radio' by Rush, and Ally could still recognize them.

CHAPTER 10

MY very good friend Anne Barrett, who I met through the music industry and was once the singer Natalie Imbruglia's manager, had sent me an Archangel Michael medallion in the post so I could put it under Ally's pillow. She was absolutely sure it would work. So under the pillow it went, joining Louisa's Padre Pio crucifix and the smoky quartz crystal. We were building quite a collection.

If the archangels really existed and had the power to help, it was certainly worth giving it everything I had. So I appealed to them quietly in the hospital chapel. Dad would talk quite loudly to them – there were all these people praying silently, and he'd be chatting with these supernatural entities for everyone to hear! I'd known about Archangel Gabriel for a long time, because I'd sung about him many times as a kid in the church choir. There was that marvellous hymn Gabriel's Message, which goes: 'The angel Gabriel from Heaven came / With wings as drifted snow, with eyes as flame'. I looked the other archangels up on the internet now, and I was ready to believe they were all around Ally, ready to fight his corner.

Why shouldn't I have believed that? When you're going through an experience as traumatic as this, when you stand to lose the one person in the world you love more than anything, all you can do is try whatever's available, which means you have to start believing in some pretty amazing things. Archangels? Sure. Crystals? Yep. Visualization? Damn right.

And who knows what power these things have when we weave them together in new combinations? We were building a powerful 'rainbow army' to come and rescue Ally.

Sceptics can laugh all they like, but would they reject all possibilities of mystical assistance if they found themselves in this situation? If I'd chosen to disbelieve in anything that might have helped the tiniest bit, I'd never have forgiven myself if Ally had slipped away.

Meanwhile, the National Hospital for Neurology & Neurosurgery were doing everything they could to mend him as well. I was spending most of my life here now, but because

I was arriving early on dark autumn mornings and leaving late and night, I was totally unaware of what a beautiful building this was. It was a red-brick Victorian job with two pointy gables and lovely tall windows, which had been built in the 1880s, back when the place was called the National Hospital for the Paralyzed and Epileptic. But Queen Square had been a place for treating mental patients long before that.

In fact, After King George III went mad in the late 18th century, he was treated somewhere here – perhaps close to the very spot where Ally was now!

On Thursday, Day 10 (2 stars), Ally had a lovely camp male nurse looking after him in the ward. Ally had been awake during the night; he hadn't been talking, but he'd been seen wiggling his fingers, though he hadn't been asked to do that. His temperature was way up again, and I pleaded with God that the vasospasms would taper off by the weekend. But I felt he was speaking and laughing with his eyes; they gave the definite impression that he knew who everyone was, and they also made me feel that he was still in love with me. But he looked confused when I asked him about being sat up the day before: he didn't remember that.

By 3pm he'd gone off the boil altogether: he was very distant, unresponsive, and I felt he wasn't understanding my words any more. It scared me, but that's how he was when he was having vasospasms. I hated the way the vasospasms were taking away the little pieces of Ally that we'd seen – the snatches of speech, the occasional movements, the look of recognition in his eyes.

They sat him up in the big chair again that day, and you could see he hated being hoisted up like that. He cried: tears streamed out of his eyes, though he made no sound, which was an incredibly sad thing to see. I couldn't bear the fact that I was powerless to help him. But I tried to be strong and I gave him a good talking to: I said he'd better not be sad, because he was still alive; also, he had a lot of work to do to get better, and the rest of us were trying to help him, and if he was crying we couldn't do the work we had to do. I was sure he was beginning to realize the state he was in. For so long he'd been in another world, oblivious to so much that was happening, and now the full horror of it was dawning on him. The senior nurse said I should leave him for a while, but there was no way I was leaving. I stayed and sang some Simon & Garfunkel to him: 'The Only Living Boy In New York', and then 'Cecilia' – he hated that song, but I thought it might move him to tell me to shut up. I needed a response of some kind, any kind.

When Kaz and Dave came in to show him Kaz's bump, his face seemed to show amazement, and I was sure that he smiled as well. But he still looked emotional and scared. On the good side, any emotion was a good thing – it showed there was some life in him.

On the car journey home, the rest of the family were talking about how bad Ally was: how he was at 'the end of his rope', how he was trying to fight but the effort was too hard for him in the weak state he was in. Back home, ready once again to try anything, I ran a cold bath, got in and did some more visualization. I didn't care about how cold I felt: that was nothing compared with what Ally was going through. Deep in freezing water, I created a visual metaphor for Ally putting his brain back in working order again.

I pictured Ally's brain as a filing cabinet. But all the files from inside it were on the floor, and he was picking them up, reading them and putting them back in the cabinet, in the right order, one by one. I was also trying to send the freezing sensation on my skin straight to him, to bring his temperature down. I concentrated so hard I felt I was nearly bursting.

An awful feeling of doom came over me then, and I didn't know why, but I decided to try to shake that off and carry on. I focused on the idea that if I could visualize something clearly, it could really happen in real life, and then I conjured an image of Ally in a running vest, with a number on it: he was running and there was a crowd of us cheering him on. But I started to lose my concentration, and that image was replaced by one I didn't want, in which he was in a wheelchair and wearing a nappy, with his tongue hanging out, dribbling. I fought against the image. 'Get out of my head! Get out!' I told it in my mind. Visualization may sound easy (and that's one of the reasons why sceptics dismiss it) but it isn't: it takes a hell of a lot of mental strength, and I was exhausted. I went to bed and slept as if I'd taken an overdose.

The next day, Day 11, didn't deserve any stars in my diary: it got a black dot instead, and I wrote the words "dark dark day". The spasms had gone from moderate to severe, and they couldn't stabilize Ally. On top of that, they were sure he'd suffered another stroke, which had taken away his motor skills and his speech, and they didn't think he'd get those back. He was totally unresponsive, though somehow he still looked as if he was fighting.

I was very scared. At 4pm, Dad and I were taken back into the little room where the staff usually delivered the bad news. They were backed into a corner, they said. They were losing him, and he couldn't fight by himself any more, so he had to go back on life support. Okay, I said – but stop talking about it and just go and do it, please. Please, quickly!

When Brenda and I looked at Ally, he was worse than ever. His eyes were closed, he he'd lost all of his colour, his temperature was back up to 40, and he couldn't breathe. He couldn't breathe! It was the second time in 11 days that I'd seen him on the brink of death. I asked the nurse if he could do something quickly. He said he'd call the doctor and we should leave now, and he pulled the curtains round Ally's bed.

I wrote in my diary: 'Back on life support with severe spasms by 8pm. Just shit.'

That night, I walked home through London in the dark with Sandra, all the way from Holborn to Hampstead and then from Hampstead to Muswell Hill, which took 3½ hours. Dave had driven Brenda and Alistair back to the bungalow, but I was desperate to get out in the open air for a while.

Part of me just wanted to run and run, and maybe jump off something. Instead I just walked and walked, picking up quite a bit of speed, working up a bit of a glow. Sandra kept up with me all the way. It was a clear night and the stars were shining down on me. Just two weeks before, Ally and I had been gazing up at the stars on holiday in Italy, lying under blankets and drinking gin-and-tonics with our friends Maggie and

Janey. I'd been so terrified the whole time of Ally having vasospasms that I'd forgotten that it was strokes that were the biggest risk at the moment – apart from death, of course. Stupid, stupid, unprepared girl!

I'd been so positive and upbeat in front of everyone at the hospital for all this time, and now here I was, having an emotional meltdown. I'd completely run out of positivity, which was so unlike me. I'm a dreamer: I'd always lived in a world where, if you wish and believe hard enough, you can do anything you want and make good anything that's bad. It's all in your hands – you're the captain of the ship.

Even as a young girl, I believed I had the power to change things using my mind. When I was about 10, a boy called Russell and two of his friends used to hang around on their bikes near our house in Barking, and Karen and I and our friend Johanna used to peep out at them through the window, and then quickly drop to the floor in case they saw us looking. Of course, they always saw us, and we were secretly pleased that they did. One day I tried an experiment: I told Karen and

Johanna that I was going to concentrate really hard and make Russell fall off his bike. I didn't want him to get hurt: I just wanted to test my supernatural powers.

They laughed and said: "Go on then, you weirdo!" So I stared and stared, I wished and concentrated as hard as I could. About 10 minutes later, Russell was sitting on his bike while leaning against the wall, with both feet on the ground, when suddenly he and his bike came crashing down.

But I wasn't the captain any more. I didn't even have a ship now – I didn't want one either. As we walked, I told Sandra that it was kinder if Ally died, because then he wouldn't have to suffer any more.

In any case, he had about two weeks of vasospasms to get through without dying, and what were the chances of that? And he'd already had two strokes, so my gut feeling that he would make a full recovery had all been shit – stupid dreams that obviously couldn't be trusted. I'd been so sure he'd come back to me, exactly as he'd been before, but I'd been an idiot to believe that.

Sandra is brilliant, she has great life-coaching skills, and she really tried to lift my spirits and make me think positively again. But I was beyond help.

As I left her at her place in Hampstead, I told her I didn't believe in God any more, that I wasn't going to bother with all that 'crystal shit', and that all the visualization and prayers were utter bollocks as well.

I said I just had to accept the truth: that despite what I'd thought, we weren't lucky people and life was just shit. I kissed Sandra and thanked her for all her support, and I promised I'd try to get back to a positive frame of mind – but added that I couldn't see it happening.

As I went to bed, crying, I swore that I didn't love God any more – I didn't care about him any more, and he could just fuck off.

CHAPTER 11

WHEN I woke up the next morning, Day 12, I was heavy with all the feelings of the night before, but full of energy – which I put down to that long walk. The day before had hit me like a ton of bricks, and I'd been totally without faith and hope. But that morning, I was more convinced than ever that we'd get Ally out of this – maybe not completely as he'd been before, but alive, and with as much 'Ally' as possible.

I decided I was going to give everything a go now, crystals and visualization and prayer and whatever else we had to do. And I'd believe in it all, not giving a toss what other people thought. We couldn't get to see Ally that morning. When we were finally allowed in at midday, Ally was in a bad way: he looked as white as a sheet and he was sweating like I didn't think possible.

They tried to impress on us once again that we could be facing the worst possible outcome here – did we understand that? Yes, we bloody do, thank you! When they took him away to test his vasospasms again, Mum, Dad, Brenda and I left the hospital and went off in different directions.

I went for a long walk on my own around Covent Garden, where I narrowly avoided an emotional encounter. I saw Sharleen Spiteri walking near Seven Dials, talking away on her mobile. I ducked out of sight before she could see me: I couldn't face having a conversation with her at this point. The members of Texas were all getting my regular round-robin texts about Ally's progress; I'd sent one the night before, telling them he wasn't good and asking them to pray for him. There was absolutely nothing else I had to say right now, because I would have crumbled so quickly in front of people.

But Mum, Dad, Brenda and I had a bit of a laugh when we got back to the hospital. When we'd separated earlier, we hadn't discussed when we'd meet up again, but there we all were, approaching the front doors at the same time, as if we'd all been summoned. They'd changed Ally's pillows, and I was upset to see that his crucifix, medallion and crystal had been placed on the side. So I wrote a message on a Post-it note, asking whoever moves him if they'd please replace the charms under his pillows.

He was still sweating so much that there was already a halo of moisture around his head on the fresh pillow. Their latest experiment was to lower his sedation a bit, to see what would happen. By now, Brenda and I had a good system going to refresh Ally's cold flannels: one of us would mop his head with a flannel, while the other went to the sink to rinse another flannel with cold water, and we'd carry on like that for hours on end. The camp male nurse we liked had started calling us "the Flannel Ladies". We agreed that if Ally could see what we were doing, he would've been mortified: he couldn't stand people fussing around him. And suddenly Brenda and I found the whole scenario hysterically funny, and we fell about laughing.

I looked closely at him as I mopped him, and that's when I saw his eyes flicker and his mouth move. Then his eyebrow spasmed, and then everything was bloody spasming. His doctors arrived to tell us that the vasospasms should have peaked, but the latest Doppler ultrasound scan of his blood vessels showed they hadn't, so they were going to keep up his hypertension for three or four more days.

Karen had insisted that we go to her place for dinner that night – she said we had to have a break from the hospital environment – so we left Ally lying there, unresponsive with a temperature of 39.8C. Dave cooked a lovely curry, though I still found it almost impossible to eat anything, and we all watched The X Factor together. Or we tried to watch The X Factor, because it was impossible to pay attention when all we could think about was getting back to the hospital to be with Ally and watch over him.

I couldn't bear the idea that Ally would wake up and look for me and I wouldn't be there. It was an intense feeling of despair and panic, and it reminded me of a cat I once had. When I was a teenager, I left home and went to live with my boyfriend at the time, Peter, in a flat in Dagenham. Our cat Sam was the most gorgeous thing; he was so affectionate, and I loved him to bits. One night he came in covered in fleas, so I got my tweezers and started pulling all these fleas out as he lay spreadeagled on my lap. When I accidentally pinched his body with the tweezers, he yelped and jumped off. I picked him up and kissed him and told him how sorry I was, but he skulked outside, and then he didn't come back.

I made Peter go and search for him, and he found Sam dead in the gutter of the main road; he'd been run over. My heart was broken, and we buried him in the field behind the flat. About a year later we'd planned to move, but I couldn't bring myself to leave the flat, because Sam was still there in the field. What if he should wake up one day and look for us, I thought, and we weren't there? I knew it was ridiculous, but I still hated the idea of Sam being all on his own there, abandoned.

Many years later, here I was, thinking: what if Ally's looking for me just before he dies, and I'm not there?

Pleasure, enjoyment and fun were all forbidden to us now. Brenda and Alistair each ate a chocolate at Karen's place, and afterwards they said they felt terrible about doing that – the idea of enjoying something like a chocolate while their son lay fighting for his life. But at least we'd all had a welcome respite from the hospital. It was a short walk home from Karen's, which was just three streets away from our bungalow. Just as we reached my road, my mobile rang. It was midnight and it was a withheld number – it didn't look good.

'Is that Mrs McErlaine?' said a voice. 'I'm afraid Alistair's lost all response. His brain-fluid drain is not draining. We've had to take him in for immediate surgery. Can you come in?' When she heard the news, Brenda collapsed right there in the street, with Alistair watching and not knowing what to do. It was too much for all of us to take, and we were hysterical.

Although it was late, I was desperate and I felt I had to text Pauline: 'please can you ask your healers to work on ally's brain drain and vasospasms, he's gone, he's not doing well, he's in surgery, I need everyone now'.

Miraculously, she texted back almost immediately. She explained that she'd been using a sponge to represent Ally's brain during the visualizations. She'd put the sponge in a glass of water, so it would absorb the water and become full, and then she'd squeeze the water out of the sponge and down the drain. She said she was squeezing the sponge and visualizing his brain right now, to help the fluid drain away.

When I saw Ally after surgery, his eyes were open but he wasn't looking at me, and he looked both scared and frustrated. They'd sedated him, because he couldn't cope with the breathing tube. But now he'd started to trigger his own breathing again, so they at 1am they took him back to surgery to remove the tube. We sat and waited again – I couldn't believe how patient I'd become in the space of two weeks.

Eventually Ally was wheeled out of the lift, still in his bed. He had an oxygen mask on but he was breathing for himself, he had a new spring on his head to keep the drain in place, and another part of his head had been shaved – so there wasn't much hair left now. His eyes were open, and although his face was less expressive, I got the impression that he was taking in his surroundings and listening to what we were saying, and that he was really pissed off. Bill had been assigned to Ally because he was a very senior nurse: Ally's condition was changing rapidly, and quick decisions had to be made. But Ally wasn't giving Bill what he needed that day: he wouldn't say anything or poke his tongue out on request.

Because it was such a quiet day and Ally just wasn't with us, I spent much of that day visualizing. I'd also brought the crystals Pauline had sent me in to the hospital to see what I could do with them. I'd heard that you could work by instinct, handling the crystals and seeing which ones present themselves most strongly to you.

So I got them all out of their little bags, and the one that really appealed to me was a piece of metallic-looking blue stuff, whose label identified it as blue tourmaline. I sat with the crystal warming up in my hand and concentrated on it, then I rubbed it on Ally's forehead and pressed it into his hand. It was completely instinctive – I didn't even know if that was what you were supposed to do, but if felt right and it felt good to do it, so I carried on, and then I put the crystal under his pillow. There was a book with the crystals, and I read that blue tourmaline is meant to be good for the brain and the immune system, for balancing the brain's left and right hemispheres, and for banishing feelings of negativity and sadness – which all sounded like what the doctor ordered! While I left the blue tourmaline with Ally, I kept a little green stone for myself, and put it in my pocket. It was a piece of howlite, which really did seem to make me feel calmer and more positive and more able to cope with everything. The crystals made me feel as if I'd found a new strength, a new source of energy.

Ally's 'rainbow army' of healers had grown now, as many of our friends made their own individual efforts to concentrate their attention on him and get him through this. Christians, Buddhists, pagans and even football players were getting involved. Johnny McElhone, the bass player in Texas, got some famous Celtic players to leave goodwill messages on Ally's phone; Big Paul, who was looking after the phone, would come in play the messages by Ally's ear. Anne Barrett put him on every church prayer list she could think of, and had hundreds of people light candles for him. We'd receive little cards saying that a candle had been lit in a particular church – everywhere from Scotland to Eastern Europe.

My writer friend Helienne, who's a practising Buddhist, asked everyone in her circle to chant for Ally. Our friend Brendan Croker, a wonderful guitarist from Yorkshire who used to play with the Notting Hillbillies, would send messages full of news and gossip in weekly instalments, with the instruction that it be read out to Ally in a thick northern accent – he was sure that would bring him round.

Our friend Tony Barrell, who interviewed Alisha's Attic twice for The Sunday Times, would regularly light a big candle and think hard about Ally while listening to a special piece of music. Tony and Ally had gone together to see the prog-rock band Yes in concert, so he chose their 15½-minute track 'Awaken' – the title seemed very appropriate under the circumstances. Everyone who loved Ally had their part to play, and play it they did. I went into the hospital chapel, putting my usual pound coin in the box there for people to donate to the cost of the candles. (All the family and lots of our friends had developed a habit – maybe a mass superstition – about doing this twice a day, and we must have raised hundreds of pounds' worth of candles! But I thought we were going to need them all.) And I said to whoever might be listening 'I'm getting him out – he'll be coming home like he was.' I stayed in the warmth of the chapel with Dad for a while, and then around 10pm we all went home feeling quite positive.

In bed that night, I concentrated hard on the idea of those vasospasms coming to an end, and on the image of Ally's brain draining by itself.

The next morning, Day 14, there was a huge crowd of medical staff around Ally's bed. They were doing the Doppler ultrasound scan for the vasospasms, and it was the first time I'd been allowed to watch.

The Doppler doc, the man in charge of the scans, scared me a bit – he reminded me of Eric Northman, the handsome Swedish vampire in the TV series True Blood. The vasospasms were still there – they showed up as a red line on a machine. Dr True Blood said he didn't know how severe they were: he had to go and compare this scan with the last one. The good news was that Ally had slept last night, and in the morning he'd shown signs of trying to speak to the staff. But they had to take him off for a brain scan now to determine what damage has been done by the vasospasms. They thought that he may have suffered a big stroke, and if the scan confirmed that, they wouldn't want to keep him hypertense any more – which meant that the vasospasms could kill him now.

All we could do was return to the waiting room, where we saw some of the people who had become familiar to us now: members of other families who are locked in a similar waiting game. You develop a special bond with these strangers, and tell them things you wouldn't tell anyone else.

Unfortunately, the big Indian family who had been chanting loudly in the chapel had lost their father. He'd been in the bed opposite Ally, with a grade-4 bleed, one grade below Ally's. They brought their father out in a bag, and his daughter, who was roughly my age, wailed and wailed. I gave her a hug, for what it was worth, and a dozen of them congregated by the lifts and held each other in grief. That was three families now, since Ally had been here, who'd lost their loved ones and who we wouldn't be seeing any more.

There were tissues scattered on the floor of the waiting room, and we knew that catching a cold wasn't an option with Ally so poorly, so Brenda and I obsessively cleaned up and sanitized everything, including the kettle and the door handles. Brenda and Alistair decided to leave the room then, but I sat for a while as if I was petrified, refusing to leave, just waiting silently to hear the news that would affect the rest of our lives. Then my fear and impatience got the better of me.

I decided I was fed up with playing by the rules and being polite, so I walked straight back into the ward, even though the curtains were drawn round the bed. And I heard a female nurse saying: 'Keep his blood pressure pushed up. His tap is fine.' Though they weren't addressing me and I knew I was in their way, I couldn't help replying: 'Does that mean he hasn't had another stroke?' The nurse looked uncomfortable with the question, because I shouldn't have been there and the staff normally sat you down to deliver important news. But I must have looked so pathetic and desperate that she replied.

'Yes,' she whispered, 'so far, no other strokes.'

So he had defied yet another of their predictions. It was a miracle. I burst into tears and ran outside. It was pouring with rain. After I turned the corner on Lambs Conduit Street, I looked through the window of a café and saw Brenda sitting there, with her head in her hands. I knocked on the glass and yelled: 'There's no other strokes!' She clapped her hand over her mouth, and her shoulders shook as she sobbed. 'I'm going to phone Dad!' I shouted.

That was when I realized I was hysterical, yelling in the street with tears streaming down my face, with no coat on in the pouring rain. I'd never imagined I would ever see myself like this. So I phoned Dad, and he said: 'I knew it, I just knew it. You wait and see – they don't know Ally, he'll not let that happen.' I don't think I'd ever felt so thrilled. Ally was still lying there like a total vegetable, with an enormous bleed on his brain and two strokes, but we were all ecstatic. When we saw

Ally again he was very subdued, not tracking anything with his eyes, but there was a moment when he seemed to laugh when a nurse called him 'Eric' by mistake.

His legs were in pneumatic boots to stop him from getting blood clots, and they made a soothing noise as they inflated every few minutes. Trying to keep up the communication we'd established, I goaded Ally into an arm-wrestling match, saying it would be the first time I'd be able to beat him. And totally unexpectedly, he reached out and pulled my arm straight down, with a grin on his face – he'd won, using the element of surprise. Then he was unresponsive again.

Noticing how dry, scaly and cracked his skin was, I ask for permission to put some hand cream on him, and they prescribed some cream I could use on his body as well. I started work on his arms and his chest, working around all the wires and tubes that surround him, which didn't frighten me any more.

On Day 15, Ally was asleep when we came in. He smelled quite bad, so I was concerned that he hadn't been washed properly, and his body hadn't been turned every few hours as it was supposed to be. Also he'd missed a physiotherapy session because they'd been unable to wake him. His left hand looked swollen, so I massaged it to try to get rid of all the fluid in it. But I wasn't allowed to do his right hand, because lifting it would have lowered his blood pressure, and they needed blood flowing to his brain while he was still having vasospasms.

While I was massaging Ally's hand and Brenda was mopping his brow, the doctor came to tell us that the vasospasms were still severe, which was unusual: they should have peaked but they hadn't. And they were very hard to treat, because they weren't just in one place: they'd spread to various places in Ally's body.

Great – wouldn't you bloody know it. I had a really gross image of the vasospasms as lots of tiny hands squeezing his bloody veins, giving them Chinese burns. I couldn't believe how well I was taking this latest bit of bad news: perhaps I'd been clobbered so much, nothing had any effect any more.

Part of me felt I should have been falling over and blubbing like a widow – the kind of scene I'd been seeing regularly in the hospital hallways – but there Brenda and I were, massaging and chatting away to Ally and still finding so many things to laugh hysterically about.

We felt bad about laughing, and we agreed that the nurses must have thought us terrible for it, but somehow that just made us laugh all the more. I paid a visit to the hospital chapel again, and put another pound coin in the collection box. I liked to sit right next to the radiator in the chapel, which was so much warmer and cosier than elsewhere. I'd fallen asleep quite a few times on the radiator with my head resting on my arms, and been woken by Dad when he'd come to look for me.

I texted Pauline, saying I really needed help with the vasospasms, as they weren't letting up, and she asked me to explain exactly what they were, so her healing circle could visualize them together and help us get rid of them. It was a Tuesday, and on Tuesday nights they'd all meet in her friend Mishka's shop in Glasgow, so it was the perfect time to get some serious healing going. They'd imagine Ally lying there in hospital, and they'd go to Mishka's crystal cabinet and take out the crystals that presented themselves most strongly to them. The crystals would be placed on a table that was lit with a candle chosen to suit the season of the year, or the current phase of the moon, and they'd all sit round the table with the lights off and their eyes closed, concentrating hard on the main issue of the day.

For instance, if we had to bring Ally's temperature down, they'd all imagine placing ice-cold things around him, blowing cold breezes on him, and the mercury in a thermometer going down. Or they'd imagine Ally looking content and happy in a room of ice, sitting on a chair made from ice. Then they'd visualize him getting up and opening the door, to reveal the frozen Arctic tundra before him.

If Ally needed help with his circulation, they'd visualize his cardiovascular system as Spaghetti Junction, that complicated motorway interchange in Birmingham, with all the traffic moving smoothly along it. They'd spend about two hours doing their visualizations, and Pauline said that if she woke up during the night, she'd do it again.

There weren't words enough to describe how grateful I was to Pauline and her friends, and I didn't give a shit if people thought it was all bollocks: I was going to stay positive, take all this marvellous energy that these people were giving me and use it as best I could.

At one point, I thought of taking a photograph of Ally so they could use that to visualize him better. But I was afraid of doing that: I didn't want to immortalize this moment if this was the last time I'd ever see him.

It reminded me of my granddad, who I absolutely adored and who died when I was nine years old.

I didn't go the funeral, because Mum didn't want me to, and years later when I asked why that was, Mum said she'd wanted me to remember him as he'd been when he'd been alive, and to only have a memory of him as happy and full of life – and that's totally the memory I have now of my wonderful granddad. For the past three days, they'd changed Ally's food drip because he'd been diabetic – as if he didn't have enough problems.

Apparently, it's common among patients who have been in critical care for a while. But when I got back to the ward, the nurse told me he was back to normal again – well, he wasn't diabetic any more, anyway. But the inside of his mouth was in a disgusting state and made me gag. There was a creamy white substance all over his tongue and his teeth, and I'd been asking the nurses for swabs to clean it, but no amount of swabbing seemed to help. I couldn't believe I was swabbing the inside of his mouth: I'd always had such a weak stomach.

I realized I was changing, becoming a stronger person in some ways, and I thought how shocked Ally would have been if he'd been able to see exactly what I was doing. We didn't get much from Ally that day: he spent much of the day sleeping, and seemed busy fighting his vasospasms, not to mention his brain damage.

When a nurse came to change his sweaty pillow, there was suddenly so much silent pain in his face, and he had a big dip in blood pressure, which caused everyone to rush in and the curtains to be pulled – the usual palaver.

So I retreated to the chapel again, and ended up sleeping for an hour. Dad came to find me, and he said Steve had arrived to talk about bills.

Oh God, I thought: for day I'd forgotten about everything to do with my normal life. I'd given Steve had my keys and we'd agreed he'd let himself in the house to open all my bills and then bring me the urgent ones.

I hadn't a clue how to access Ally's money to pay his personal bills, and although I knew we both put the same amount in our joint bank account every month, I thought he did that online rather than having a direct debit for it. I was so glad Steve had come, because at least I could give him my chequebook, sign the cheques that had to be signed, and make a list of the other matters I'd have to sort out soon. Reality felt as if it was spiralling out of control; I didn't have a grip on anything any more. And if I was going to be left on my own, I knew I had to take control and get it all sorted before I was buried under a pile of bills and debts, everything from income tax to car and house insurance.

CHAPTER 13

I WAS missing Ally so much now that it was starting to really hurt. For so long he'd been the first person I'd turn to in any unusual situation, and I desperately wanted to phone him and tell him what was going on. In the hospital we'd seen brief, tantalizing flashes of Ally as he used to be, and that only made me want to have him back again, all of him.

Back at the hospital on the morning of Day 18, I covered my hands with antibacterial gel, took a deep breath and swung open the door to the ward. There was Bed 4, in the corner, but it was empty. He wasn't in his bed! I panicked and broke the tense silence in the critical-care ward by crying loudly: 'Where's Ally?! Where's my husband?! Please, please, where is he?!'

I was escorted outside and told the news: during the night he'd stopped responding completely and his temperature had spiked at 40.5.

'What?!' I said. 'You've got to be kidding me!'

He'd been doing so well the day before, when he told us he was in 'a big bed in space', and now we were right back to square one again.

The lift doors opened then, and out came Ally in his bed with all the paraphernalia around it, accompanied by three nurses, who wheeled him back into the ward. He looked bad – in fact, he looked dead; there was no sign of life at all there. I took out the Celtic-green flannel, soaked it in freezing-cold water and mopped and mopped his face in the hope that it would have some effect, but it didn't. They said they suspected he had pneumonia, so they took an x-ray of his chest, and asked me to leave the room while they did that. They also brought the True Blood Doppler doctor back to do another scan for vasospasms.

So the waiting game began once more: we wouldn't know until 2pm, when all the tests came back, if he'd had another stroke, or if he was brain-dead.

I just wanted him to be alive; if he was alive, I felt we could beat the pneumonia or whatever other ailments he had. My body felt like it was constricting with pain. I took myself off again for a walk around some old haunts in Soho and Covent Garden, and I thanked God for London – all that life still going on, all that energy, like a giant wheel with countless cogs in it, perpetually turning.

Somehow that London energy was helping me, keeping me going through all the trauma. I realized then that if Ally had been put in a hospital in the suburbs or in the country, I would surely have died, let alone Ally.

When I was little, I'd constantly dreamed about living right in the middle of Covent Garden, maybe in a little attic flat with a tiny roof terrace, so I could overlook all the goings-on. I imagined I might live round the corner from Langley Street, so I could pop in and out of Pineapple Dance Studios and be fabulous. Mum used to take Karen and me 'up west' for dance classes every Saturday when we were little, and we absolutely loved it. I felt like I was in Fame, the 1980 movie I still had that feeling whenever I passed by there, and I'd seriously thought about taking classes again.

When Ally and I had first met, I'd tried to talk him into coming dancing with me. I thought it would be fun to do something Latin and sexy with him, like salsa, but he wasn't keen. I reasoned that as a guitarist he'd have great coordination, but I couldn't have been more wrong. I'd seen him dance once at a wedding, and I remember standing at the edge of the dance floor with four other girls as we watched in disbelief at the shapes he was making with his body.

He played a gig with Texas once at the Town & Country Club in Kentish Town, and he actually tripped over his own foot while he was trying to bust a move, which sent him tumbling backwards into the drum kit! When it came to dancing, I'd stopped encouraging him to partake. There was a good reason why he used to stay at the bar whenever we went to a wedding.

After walking for two hours, I returned to the hospital at 2pm to find he machines bleeping like crazy: Ally's heart rate was up to 180 and his blood pressure was scarily low. He was shaking violently, with his eyes rolling back into his head. It was just like the day when this had all started, when the medics were trying to make him breathe before they'd rushed him off to hospital. The senior nurse was usually so composed but now he looked scared. He went off to reception to use the phone, turning his back on us so we didn't know what he was saying, and after about five minutes he returned and started injecting Ally very quickly with all sorts of stuff.

There were suddenly five critical doctors round the bed, chattering about what to do. It was all happening so fast, it was a bit of a blur. They couldn't find a reason for Ally's high temperature. He didn't have pneumonia or any chest infection – they said it would be easier if he had, because at least then they could treat it.

They started talking about putting him back on life support, and then I heard the senior nurse say to them: 'He's got to fight this if he's still breathing for himself.'

Ally was shaking so violently, totally freaking out, that I thought – how many times had I thought this so far? – that we might be losing him now.

All I could do was hold his legs down, in an effort to control the terrible shaking. But the latest scans showed that there were no more strokes, so that was great news. But there was still something wrong that they couldn't find. I suggested that they check his ears, because he sometimes had ear infections; that was his Achilles' heel, which is quite unfortunate for a musician.

So one of the doctors checked and said: 'No, there's no infection – but he's growing some potatoes in there!' I laughed, and realized how strange it sounded: it was the first time I'd laughed that day. They took his brain drain out, because they wanted to test the end of the tube that was going into his brain for any infections. Every time they'd tried to take it out before, he'd lost all response, and they'd had to put it back again so he wouldn't have another stroke. I hoped he was ready this time.

There was no let-up that day, and I was exhausted by 10pm when we left. Ally was still unstable and burning up, so they didn't wash him, as they would normally have done. But there was good news about the young Brazilian woman in the next bed to Ally's. I'd see her husband quite often and catch up with their story – hear how she'd twitched an eyebrow or opened her eyes for the first time – and today she'd left the critical-care unit for another ward; she'd been taken off the critical list, which was fantastic.

There was more drama with Ally on Day 19. They'd found some cultures in his blood, and the antibiotics they'd started him on yesterday weren't working, so they'd decided to change them. He must have been like a human medicine cabinet by now.

Today they renewed all his arterial lines, and while that gave me some hope – someone must have believed that he was going to be here for a bit longer, at least – I felt so sorry for him: it was all so invasive, and he'd always hated people seeing his body.

I'd never seen him pee until we were nine years into our relationship, and even then he was mortified. I decided as they were renewing all his tubes, I'd renew all his flannels as well, so I went round to Boots and bought six new ones – three white and three green, keeping our loyalty to Celtic going.

Ally woke for just five minutes today, that was all, and I was massaging his arm when it happened. He said something I couldn't quite make out, which sounded like: 'This is shocking.' I asked him: 'Did you say "This is shocking"?' And he mumbled a reply which sounded like: 'I said something similar.'

The nurses kept talking about 'inappropriate responses', and I told Brenda I really wanted to look through his charts and see what inappropriate answers they'd written down, because they didn't have time to tell us everything he'd said or done.

So I started going through them, but the nurse became very haughty and said: 'We don't encourage friends and family to do that!' 'Good idea!' I replied sarcastically, and defied her by continuing to look through the charts.

Brenda started laughing, which made me start as well, and pretty soon we were both falling about. The nurse was still not amused.

I really didn't like the idea of Mum and Dad driving all the way down from Milton Keynes to Muswell Hill and then to the hospital every day. On Day 20, which was a Sunday, I insisted that they take a day off. Dave drove us in again that day. I still wasn't in the right state of mind to drive myself – there didn't seem to be any room in my brain for anything other than what was happening with Ally.

Ally was sleeping a lot, not doing anything on command, and he was having problems because he was still unable to swallow. Like he was holding his breath for a short time whenever he coughed, which sounded scary. He'd occasionally come back to Earth for a few seconds, and I'd noticed that you could tell when it was going to happen: he'd flex his left hand, and two seconds later he'd open his eyes. As soon as I was left alone with him, I told him it was really important for him to say my name out loud so I could hear it – I just needed some reassurance that he still knew who I was – but he wasn't able to do that. One of the doctors who saw him when he first arrived at the hospital was here, and he talked to us and answered our questions for about five minutes. We'd saved up so many questions, several days' worth, because we'd had all these discussions in the waiting room and at home about what we needed to ask, but we usually didn't get a chance to ask them because Ally was always in the middle of some kind of emergency. The doctor said that statistically, Ally shouldn't have been alive now, and the fact he was still hanging on was a kind of miracle. They'd told us before that the vasospasms would probably be over after 14 days, and our countdown was up now: he'd fought those bastards for 14 days. The trouble was, they seemed to be continuing. There was one bit of good news, though: his infection count had come down. He was still horribly ill, but not quite as horribly ill as he'd been yesterday.

On Day 21, they did a lumbar puncture and found that Ally had an infection in his spinal fluid: they said it should be clear, but it was really thick and milky. They explained they'd have to take him straight into theatre to have another brain drain put in. The operation could go seriously wrong and cause a massive stroke. His temperature was 39.9 and he still had severe vasospasms; in fact, it was the longest episode of vasospasms they'd ever known.

Oh, terrific. It was like some horrendous black comedy: I couldn't imagine what else could go wrong. In my diary I wrote 'Docs said yesterday would be the end of vasospasms – not fucking true.' Ally had to be as sterile as possible before he went into surgery, so a lovely young blonde nurse said she was going to wash his hair. She said she couldn't believe he was so young and in such a state. She'd never known a grade-5 case to survive.

She said it would have been too distressing for Ally in his condition to have his lungs cleared with a suction tube, so she was trying to make him cough with the apple juice and then suctioning his mouth. In the end she didn't get to wash his hair, because they wanted to get him straight into theatre; there was no time to lose.

I said goodbye to his bed, and just as it started descending in the lift I got a phone call from another part of the hospital, telling me the risks of the op and the statistics of him not coming out alive, and asking for my consent. I panicked and suddenly forgot how to breathe again. I realized I'd signed his life away five times by this point. I went to the chapel again and spent a lot of time just staring at the Jesus figurine, with his arms open wide and his lovely calm face. A big family of about 20 Asian people came in, sat in a circle and started chanting – quite softly at first but gradually getting louder and louder. It sounded lovely.

Dad came to find me, and told me Ally was out of surgery and back on life support. Dad started shouting angrily and swearing up at the dome of the chapel again. I told him not to, but he said: 'Don't you worry – He knows me, He knows what I'm about.' I realized we were all cracking up a bit by now; who could blame us?

Back in Bed 4 by the window again, Ally looked dead. His hair was shaved again and the brain drain was fixed to his head again. It felt like we'd gone a few weeks back in time, back to square one, except that the weather had turned noticeably: it was getting colder, and the summer and our Italian holiday seemed like years ago now.

Ally still had a little reminder, a red triangle of T-shirt tan on his chest. When he was first on life support, one of the nurses had said: 'Don't worry about that colour on his chest – sometimes the steroids do that.' I laughed because I could imagine Ally saying: 'No, that's my tan, love!'

Suddenly he woke up, gagging, with his eyes bulging, and the blonde nurse started shining lights in his eyes and asked us to leave right away. I was so scared for him – I thought perhaps he'd reached his limit now and wouldn't be able to take any more of this suffering. I felt that he was fighting because I'd told him to fight, but that he might be causing himself enormous harm by doing it. We were at the end of our tether now, and maybe the kindest thing would be to let him go now. So before I left the ward I said this quietly in his ear: 'I've asked you to fight all these days now, I've been on and on at you – "Fight! Don't give up! You can do it!" Well, I think I want you to stop now. I can't watch it any more, and I don't think it's fair for you to have this struggle. If you have to go, you have to go, and I'll never be mad with you for it.'

Then I cried my eyes out. I went into the hallway, where all the Pooles and McErlaines were scattered about, waiting expectantly, and I explained to Dad that I'd told Ally to give up, to let go, and that I thought it was the best thing for him now. What sort of future was he likely to have now, anyway? Richard Hammond had said that there'd been that easy, peaceful road that had been so appealing, but that he could hear his wife telling him to wake up, and that was the hard road he didn't want to go down. Maybe the hard road was the right choice now.

Dad asked me if I was absolutely sure. 'He hears you, you know,' he said. And I was instantly terrified that I'd done the wrong thing telling him to give up, and if he died now it would be my fault, because I'd told him to. I flung open the doors, dashed back into the ward and pulled back the curtains. I was immediately told off, but I didn't care. I got really close to his ear again, and this time I said: 'Don't you fucking dare give up!

I was wrong. You're not going anywhere. Fight or I'll fucking kill you!! I love you so much, and I'm not having it any other way. Do you hear me?'

I must have sounded like a hysterical lunatic: I was shouting and crying and almost laughing at the same time. I just hoped he'd heard me, and that I hadn't said it too late, that he hadn't already started to throw in the towel.

Shortly after that, he started breathing for himself and triggering his life support again. The nurses couldn't believe it; they were smiling and saying 'Wow.' The blonde nurse said it wasn't too traumatic removing the tube this time, and now he looked as if he was smiling. I watched him sleep then, and after a while he woke up and I saw he was crying: there were tears coming out of his eyes, though he wasn't making a noise. I felt so sad for him and so frustrated at our inability to communicate. He couldn't tell me what he was feeling, and I couldn't make it better for him because I wasn't even sure he could hear me talking to him. I told him he was going to be absolutely fine, because I'd make sure of it – I'd do everything he needed me to do.

I said I'd love him however he came out of this, whatever he looked like. I said he could give up music if he found it was too stressful for him. And I reminded him that I was never wrong and that he was always lucky – and I swore I saw him give a little smirk at that. It was all true about him being lucky.

I'd always told people that if you ever want to win any money, take Ally into the betting shop with you. My grandad on Dad's side owned a bookie's in the East End of London, and now Dad would take us to a betting shop every now and again to put money on the horses, to keep up the old tradition. And Ally would always, always, always pick the winning horse. I'd lost count of the weird and fluky shots he'd pulled off in golf and snooker – the amazing holes-in-one and the shots that bounce 25 times round the table and land in the pocket. We'd joked about it so often, but it was true: he was a lucky man. There'd been many a moment when he'd been ridiculously close to a disaster – when a bus had missed him by a hair's

breadth and he'd walked away completely unscathed.

CHAPTER 14

THE next day, Day 22, they said he'd had a rough night; he hadn't been able to sleep. They said he had 'intensive-care psychosis'. I was sure the rest of us had that too!

Ally was doing these gigantic arm movements, which we hadn't seen before. He was doing them even when he was asleep. His body was basically paralyzed, so they said it had to be a kind of reflex. He'd occasionally wake up and then bring his right arm up to his face to try to remove the oxygen mask, with this huge gormless grin on his face. Or he'd try to pull his gown down, or yank out the tubes going into his groin. He seemed confused, so I tried to explain really slowly where he was and what was happening: 'Darling, you've had a bleed to the brain. You're in the hospital. You've been here for three weeks.'

His face took on an astonished look for a moment, and then he started trying to yank out the tubes going into his groin again. I tried to restrain his hand and I massaged it, finger by finger, and touched my face with it. Although he didn't respond at all to the nurses today, he did speak to me and Brenda. We wanted him to know we were here, so we kept the conversation going by his bed.

As Brenda and I talked, Brenda reminded me that Ally's cousin Gerald had contracted swine flu a few days before, and I said, 'Oh, did he? Wow, that must've just fallen out of my head.' And, quick as a flash, Ally said in his robotic voice: 'Oh, it must've fallen out of mine too.' Brilliant, I thought, and I decided to keep this spontaneous communication going.

'Ally, who's Martin O'Neill?' I asked him – not in a way that sounded like I was testing him, but in a curious way, as if I didn't know and wanted him to help me with the information. And, with his eyes staring blankly ahead, he replied: 'The old manager of Celtic.' Correct!

'Shall I bring you in some music?' I asked him. 'Yes,' he whispered. 'Do you want any visitors tonight?' 'No.' I felt as if he was with us for a long time that night – more than 20 minutes – but unfortunately the nurse didn't see any of this, so she marked him '0 0 0 0', as well as making a note that his temperature was boiling over.

Ally had been in critical now for so long, we'd become familiar faces to a lot of people at the National Hospital for Neurology & Neurosurgery. The nurses knew us, the doormen knew us, and even the cleaners knew us. We'd made friends with a lot of families who were in the same boat, experiencing similar levels of terror to ours. There was a mum who had two daughters, and the younger daughter, Charlotte, was in the ward next door to Ally. Charlotte had had an awful accident that had given her a massive head injury, and she wasn't able to move at all. Her sister had written something nice in the chapel prayer book – 'Please pray for Ally so he can play the guitar again' – and I'd been praying for Charlotte.

On the morning of Day 23, the top of Ally's bed was tilted upwards, which was usually a sign that he'd had a good night. But I'd become so used to bad news following good, I was waiting for a huge disappointment. He was losing a lot of weight. He was still wearing those pneumatic boots to prevent thrombosis, but every now and then I'd take them off so I could massage his legs, which were shocking to see, because they looked like thin twigs.

His speech therapist arrived and asked Ally where he was, and he looked around with a dazed and gormless expression. "Wembley Stadium?" he ventured. I explained to Sue that he may have thought he was playing a gig, and she laughed.

As soon as she left, the physiotherapists turned up, which was another good sign: they must have thought he was stabilizing if they felt it was okay to do some physio on him. I'd seen them other critical patients being sat up and thumped on the back by the physios so their fluids would move, and I'd wanted Ally to have that treatment, but so far he'd never been well enough. It took four of them to sit him up – he was like a huge floppy sandbag. So many of his muscles had wasted and he could hardly move anything – he couldn't even hold his own head up.

As they did physiotherapy on his feet and hands, I left the ward quietly to let them get on with it. I went into the loo and had a massive cry. Seeing Ally so incapable and being pulled about had been so incredibly sad to watch, and it had suddenly hit home how damaged he really was. He didn't wake again for the whole day after that. He must have been knackered – that physio must have been like climbing Everest for him.

When they started to wash him, Brenda and I went off to the nearby Brunswick Shopping Centre in Bloomsbury. We went into Waitrose, and as Brenda stood for a moment in a bit of a daze with her shopping trolley, a woman with a young child tutted loudly and said she was blocking the way – which she wasn't – and called her an idiot. At first I apologized, but then I realized how unnecessarily rude this woman had been, and it made me so angry. I lost the plot and started shouting at her: 'Yuck! What is it? Is it a woman? You must have to work really hard at being that ugly! Yuck, I literally can't look at it! Get it away from me! Eurghhh, ugly, get away!'

The rant made me feel better, but I thought I would have felt even better if I'd punched her. I'd never call a total stranger an 'idiot' for looking slightly dazed in a supermarket. How do you ever know what someone you've never met is going through? That woman had absolutely no idea what kind of life Brenda was enduring at that moment – that her son was facing death and going through countless agonies in hospital. How dare she assume that we were living perfectly normal, happy lives, and that Brenda had just stopped for a few seconds with her trolley because she was 'an idiot'? That was a massively ignorant, inconsiderate, stupid and selfish thing to do – *she* was the idiot, and she was such an idiot that didn't even know that! On the way back to the hospital, Brenda and I kept laughing about what I'd said, but I still had an urge to go back and confront the ugly bitch in Waitrose again. The lovely Dr Silverhair was a sight for sore eyes after that.

My friend Sandra and I had developed a funny little crush on him. He'd given us some of the grimmest speeches we'd ever heard – telling us all about the horrors of brain damage, frontal-lobe strokes and vasospasms – but I felt he'd helped to save Ally and was willing him to recover. He also rode a motorbike and came in wearing his leathers most mornings. If we'd known him in another time and place, I was sure we would have hung out with him as a friend.

He asked me how I was doing and I said: 'Great. I know he'll get better.' He told me he'd never met anyone quite like me, and I had to look after myself. Then he told me he'd seen a programme about Edwyn Collins on television the night before, and as he talked about it he had a little tear in his eye. He said it was really good to see people after they'd recovered and see what happened to their lives. I resolved to invite him and the other staff here to a gig if Ally got through this and started playing again, so they could see what they'd achieved. I asked Dr Silverhair what would happen next if Ally got through these next couple of days and was stable. He replied that he'd have to go into a rehabilitation unit, where he'd relearn what he could and learn to live with the disabilities he was left with. The girls upstairs in the rehabilitation unit were amazing, he said: they worked wonders.

As he left, he added 'I wouldn't be surprised if you're wheeling him round the park next week,' which was a lovely thing to say. Brenda had been off work for nearly a month now, and we'd been discussing when she'd have to go back. Her boss had been amazing, but at some point real life had to continue.

On the other hand, under no circumstances could she leave while Ally's life was in the balance, so we agreed that if and when he got off the critical list, or we could take him outside and he could feel the air on his face, she'd go back home. I danced into the waiting room to tell everyone what the lovely doctor had said, and we all cried together at the prospect of being to take Ally to the park.

Sometimes I'd sit in the park by myself when they were washing him, and I'd look at the patients who were having a taste of the outdoors after being in hospital for so long. Many of them didn't seem to have much of a clue where they were or what was happening, but they still seemed to be relishing the fresh air.

Ally had always loved feeling the breeze on his skin. He'd keep a bedroom window open even in freezing weather, and open doors to air the house. I knew he'd love to be outside and away from the bright strip lighting and the noisy rubbish bins that went 'Clang!' every time they closed after a used paper towel was put in.

I was so excited by the idea of Ally alfresco, I realized I might have been on an even bigger high now than when I first saw the wonderful Neil Diamond play at Birmingham NEC from the front row of the stalls! Back to reality again: Ally had some more infections, including one in his blood, and as we left the hospital that day, his temperature was up again. But they'd taken his oxygen mask off and I was able to actually kiss his mouth. And I felt like he was stable for the first time since that terrible day, September 8.

I knew how things could change in a heartbeat, so I tried not to let my emotions run away with me. But how could I do that when I was so elated? I'd always felt I was lucky too, but the difference between me and Ally was that I'd had to work really hard for everything I'd got: I'd had to fight for things and be the one to make things happen. Meanwhile, Ally would just fall into things; great situations would somehow gravitate towards him. He hadn't needed to put much effort into things to be good at them, which had been bloody annoying at times, if I'm honest.

I realized that this was the one time in his life when he was actually going to have to fight hard for himself. We couldn't do it for him: we could give him all our love and our wishes and our positive energy, but this was his personal battle now. And if he really was born lucky, he needed that luck more than he'd ever needed it before, because his whole life was at stake now.

I was being reminded regularly now by every doctor, nurse and consultant I saw that even if he survived he would be mush, basically: there wouldn't be anything remaining of the Ally that I knew and loved. He would be severely brain-damaged and disabled for the rest of his life, and I'd be his full-time career.

But I was trying not to think about that: I'd cross that bridge when I came to it. First of all I just wanted him to live, and once he'd done that, I'd deal with all the rest of it the crap I had to deal with afterwards.

CHAPTER 15

IT was October now, and the weather had turned freezing cold. Ally was still in Bed 4 in critical care, because of his high temperature and racing heart rate. The rest of his body seemed to be stabilizing, though he still couldn't swallow, and his body would shake violently about twice a day and have to be held down.

Every now and then the machines would go into bleeping overdrive, but I'd seen it all now and it didn't frighten me as much as it had before. They regularly took him out of bed and into that big chair, which they said was like an intense kind of physiotherapy: though the chair had braces to hold his head, neck and torso, he had to use a lot of muscles to perform the simple task of sitting up. He'd sit with a strained expression, just staring ahead, and after that he'd be asleep for about 10 hours in his bed.

We still didn't know exactly how brain-damaged he was, but in those occasional moments when he spoke he certainly sounded confused. At one point, while he was gazing into space, I asked him what he was thinking. 'I'm thinking about the box with all the blue stuff in it,' he replied.

A bit later, he informed Dad and me that he could see 'giant cut-out strawberries'. 'I think you're dreaming, honey,' I said. 'Shhh!' he replied. 'I'm looking to see if that guy in the doorway is a Celtic supporter.' There was no guy in the doorway. But he had some self-awareness: when the speech therapist asked him if he was hallucinating, Ally said yes. 'Where do you think you are?' she asked. 'The departure lounge,' he replied. He was certainly getting about.

The psychologist here said it was better not to correct him, because that would make him more confused, but I couldn't help correcting him sometimes, because it instinctively seemed the better thing to do. It was upsetting to think he was becoming more and more deluded – how could that be a good thing? Mum had printed off hundreds of photographs now, and I was using them as test cards, showing them to him to see if he recognized anything. He recognized our friends, and

Casper, who was a dog we played with on our holidays in Scotland. He could tell you his name and his date of birth if you asked him now. He knew the name Brenda too, but he seemed to think that was my name. I'm sure Sigmund Freud would have had a field day with that one.

'No, Ally, what's your **wife**'s name?' asked the nurse. 'Brenda,' he'd say. 'No, her! That lady there, your wife.' 'Brenda!' Then he'd look at us as if **we** had gone mad. He didn't know where we lived, my birthday (March 20) or what kind of car I had – but then he'd never liked my Smart Car, so I suspected he'd blanked that out on purpose. I asked him what band he was in, and he said 'Texas.'

When I showed him pictures of our band Red Sky July, he didn't seem to know the name of the band, but he gave a huge smile and said 'Charity.' I told him I'd heard from Grace Maxwell, the wife of the singer Edwyn Collins. Ally had been a big Orange Juice fan, and he'd been devastated when Edwyn had suffered a massive stroke in 2005. Of course, Ally had had no idea then that he would collapse himself four years later – although what happened was quite different from what had happened to Edwyn. Grace had seriously been through the mill with Edwyn's recovery, and I'd felt a strong connection with her and contacted her by email.

'I got a lovely reply back from Grace today,' I said, almost certain that nothing of this was registering with him. 'She's been through the kind of thing I'm going through now. That's Edwyn Collins' wife, Ally, do you remember who he is?' Ally replied 'Ooh, funny you should mention Edwyn. I saw him climbing up the outside of the building this morning.' What a marvellous image. I was pretty sure that Edwyn Collins hadn't really turned into Spider-Man to pay Ally a visit.

In the end, I came out with the usual rubbish response of: 'Oh my God, did you just speak?! *Nurse, he just spoke!*' At which point he went back into a daze and it all went quiet again. But, I said to myself, he knows who Edwyn is. That was good.

While he could be quite chatty with us, he was often totally gormless and silent when the doctors were with him, so sometimes I'd call them over when he spoke, just to show them the progress he was making. At times he reminded me of a ventriloquist's dummy: mostly he'd be staring blankly ahead with his tongue hanging out slightly, but occasionally he'd pipe up with a short comical remark from his confused mind. There were times when I hardly recognized him at all. He looked terribly forlorn, in such a sorry state, with his shaved head and the Frankenstein bolts attached to it. There were massive bedsores on his bum and legs, which were now accompanied by nasty rashes from the two big plasters that held his food tube in place ever since he'd started pulling the tube away during the night.

I'd tried to stay away from the internet, which can turn you into a hypochondriac lunatic if you're not careful, but I couldn't help looking up the known effects of frontal-lobe strokes. I did it every night in the desperate hope that it might read differently, but it was always the same.

He was likely to lose motor skills, problem-solving skills, cognition and intellect. He might be paralyzed, incontinent, and prone to mood swings, inappropriate remarks, and repetitive reflexes such as sucking, groping and mimicking people's facial expressions.

Then there was the killer bit, about how his personality could be totally changed. I loved him so much, and I just couldn't cope with the idea of him losing his great personality, and gaining a new one that I wouldn't necessarily like.

As I ran all these horrific ideas through my head, I tried not to picture myself behind a wheelchair, pushing a nutty old man with his pants on his head who kept shouting 'Bugger' at strangers, but that image wouldn't leave me alone.

By October 3, Day 26, Ally had been having vasospasms for 20 days.

They'd kept him hypertense to ensure he had enough blood going to the brain, and because of the risks of that, they'd installed a cardiac-arrest alarm button next to his bed. But the doctors said the vasospasms were tapering off now, they'd gone from severe to moderate, so they decided to use drugs to bring down his blood pressure, from 180 over 100 to 160 over 96. This was a momentous day, and I breathed a huge sigh of relief.

The nurse asked him how he was feeling, and he suddenly sounded very eloquent and medically knowledgable. 'I'd say heightened sensitivity all over,' he said.

Earlier today, his speech therapist had held up a pen and asked him what it was, and he'd said 'A dog,' which was pretty disappointing, so now I was excited to let her know he was making more sense and had some new words.

I tried to call her on an internal phone, but there was no answer. I'd decided that I wanted him back as he was before, that I couldn't accept anything less than that, so I'd been making lists of things that might trigger his mental recovery.

That day, I'd brought one of his favourite books in, a volume of pictures by the film director and photographer Wim Wenders.

Dad and I looked through it and deliberately had a long conversation about it by Ally's bed. His eyes were closed, so we made sure we described the book and mentioned Wim

Wenders' name. 'Ooh, these are gorgeous,' I said. 'I wonder when these were taken.'

'I don't know, Shell,' whispered Ally, with his eyes still shut, 'in the 1960s...?' Of course, he was right.

Music was going to play an important role too. Grace Maxwell had emailed me to say that it was only when Edwyn got back to making music that he really felt right again. I'd been nervous of playing Ally music for a long time, because I'd been worried about his poor head. But now the bag on the end of his brain drain didn't look so full of blood, so the headphones came out. Gram Parsons, Cat Power and Bob Dylan didn't know it, but they had some serious work to do here.

The next day, I got up early to go straight to the hospital as usual. This was virtually all I did now: I still wasn't eating, and all the things my body was supposed to be doing seemed to have stopped; it was as if Ally and I were suspended in time. Some flowers arrived at the house with a gorgeous card from Dougie (the Rush record-breaker) and his wife Tina on behalf of Ally, wishing me a happy wedding anniversary. Of course! It was October 5, the day we got married eight years before. I wanted to get something for Ally to celebrate our special day, but it would have been meaningless to him in his current state, and that made me feel a pang of sadness.

He'd said quite a few words by now, and he knew people's names and the name of one of the bands he was in, but, if I was realistic, he still hadn't really returned to us. He was just a big piece of jelly, really, with a few random and sporadic flickers of intelligence here and there, which he appeared to have no control over. He was just one notch above brain-dead. He was unable to keep eye contact, and the responses he gave were few and far between – six or seven hours apart. When he said something it was such a shock, because it came from someone who was so removed and apart from the world. But that didn't mean it didn't cheer me up enormously whenever he spoke.

I'd be thinking 'Can I handle nursing him? Can I make the sacrifices I have to make without wanting to chuck myself under a bus?' and then he'd smile into the distance and say something daft in that robot voice, like: 'The kitchen's steaming up,' and I'd be deeply in love with him again.

hen we arrived at the hospital, Ally was lying flat on his bed with his neck in a very crooked position, but he was speaking straight away. I asked him if he was still confused, and he answered 'I'm still confused' with that familiar blank stare. He also said 'Hello, Mum' to Brenda, which was marvellous.

We had to leave the ward then, and we spent a lot of time waiting because they were doing ward rounds, and after that the Doppler doc came to test him for vasospasms again. But when we returned, his nurse told us that the doctors and consultants were very happy with him, and maybe after two days of being weaned off the noradrenaline they were using to keep him hypertense for the vasospasms, he could move out of critical care and into the high-dependency unit next door.

We knew it meant that they didn't fear for his life any more, which was fantastic, and I jumped for joy.

It was Brenda and Alistair's last day, because Brenda had to go back to work, which meant I was shortly going to be on my own in the house, and I didn't know how I felt about that. Brenda and Alistair said goodbye around 5pm before making their way back to Scotland. Ally said: 'See you next weekend' to them for some reason, and was blissfully unaware of his mother crying as she walked out the door.

When I saw Dr Silverhair in the hall, I asked if he thought I could have Ally home by February, in whatever state he'd be in then. And he said that at this rate, he might even be able to make a home visit by Christmas. I almost fainted when I heard that – I actually felt my legs begin to collapse under me. So it was just me by Ally's big chair that afternoon, feeling a bit lonely. When he woke, I mopped his sweaty head, changed his sweaty pillow and picked a bit of congealed blood off his hair – yuk!

I massaged all his fingers and tried to lift his legs twice to get his fluids moving, but the arterial lines got in the way. Then at 6pm he was back in the big blue hoist, being lifted back into bed. They'd told me to keep him awake if I could during the day, because if he slept he was likely to be awake at night and would have to be sedated; he needed to maintain a normal day/night routine. So I got a lot of music out to stop him from nodding off – 'Metal Heart' by Cat Power, 'That's the Way' by Led Zeppelin, 'Mr Bojangles' sung by Neil Diamond. I read him a chapter of Moby Dick as well.

The day was fast approaching when Ally would be moved, and it was going to be weird after all this time in Bed 4, because this had felt like a safe place, with Ally being watched round the clock. I'd even got used to the stark lighting. When he moved out of critical to HD ('high dependency' – or 'high definition', as we were calling it), he'd have to share a nurse with another patient.

It was on the Day 29, October 6, that the consultants decided Ally was breathing well enough for himself now and should move out of critical. So five nurses began to move his bed, together with all his tubes, his pillow charms and his other paraphernalia, into high dependency. I trailed behind with a wheelchair stacked with all his photographs, books, flannels and toiletries – it was a bit like moving house. I got quite emotional with all the lovely nurses who had tended to his every need for the best part of a month. I couldn't say enough thank-yous; it was like a long movie goodbye.

I turned to take a long look at the room that had been home for so long, the place where we'd been locked in time, and tears rolled down my cheeks as I hoped I wouldn't ever see it again.

The HD room was all blue, with huge windows looking onto the outside world. Great, I thought: hopefully, there'd be some real life to watch here. Ally was just staring straight ahead, and I wondered if he'd realized that he was in a different place now. It was much quieter, with just the two of us and one nurse at the desk. They'd told me he probably wouldn't be here for long: although his heart rate was still very high, they wanted to get him up to a proper ward as soon as they could – the Victor Horsley ward, named after a great scientist who once worked at the hospital. They suggested I go and take a look at it, but I was dreading it, because I can't bear those hospital wards with long lines of beds and weird Alan Partridge hotel curtains.

So Sandra went first to do a recce for me. She came back saying: 'Oh dear, Shell, you're going to hate it!' Then Paul and Steve went up, and when they returned Paul said: 'No, it's great. It's absolutely fine.' But I could see Steve looking a little worried, because he knew exactly what I could and couldn't cope with. Leaving Paul, Sandra and Steve with an unresponsive Ally, I went to see for myself.

It looked horrible, and it smelled like a nasty combination of public toilets and airline food. There were four beds on each side, with each patient directly facing somebody else. The curtains were yellow and blue, and the beds had crisp white sheets with old-lady mustard-coloured blankets on them. There was a switch to move the bed up and down, and a button for summoning a nurse. I wasn't being snobby – I'm from the East End of London, for heaven's sake – but I felt that we'd worked so hard and made so much of our lives as musicians, and my first reaction was that Ally was just too good for this. It was so not the kind of environment I could ever see us in.

Up to this point, Ally's treatment had been provided by the National Health Service, but we had private medical insurance as well, and I felt that this was the time we should start using it. I went into a panic and started doing a kind of crying dance – 'Oh, dear God! I can't put him in there. I can't. I can't! I want to put him in a private hospital – now!' Dr Silverhair saw me freaking out in the hallway and stopped me to have a word. We should really keep Ally on the NHS, he said: the NHS had worked with him from the start of all this, they knew him and knew his specific needs really well, and he was going to be needing a lot of medical assistance from now on. It wasn't what I'd wanted to hear. He added, in quite a casual, chatty way: 'You're going to have to do lots of physio with him yourself, you know – they don't get much time up there.'

Back at Ally's bedside, a bunch of us sat and discussed his fate. But our conversation was interrupted by a bit of a commotion, as the doors swung open and a bed trundled through. It was one of my new friends from the waiting room – Shirley, with her husband Anthony, who had Guillain-Barré syndrome; his whole system had closed down and he couldn't do anything for himself. He had a trach, a tube in his throat to help him breathe. I'd heard the whole story from our chats in the waiting room and she'd heard mine, and it was lovely to finally see the man himself.

'And this is Ally,' I said, introducing my blank-faced husband, with his tongue hanging slightly out, and Shirley gave me a sad look. She said that they'd found the notorious hospital bug MRSA in the ward where Anthony was, so they'd moved everyone out and were giving the place a thorough clean. 'MRSA, that's all we need,' I said, remembering that Edwyn Collins had that on top of his awful stroke and it had nearly bloody killed him. I'd had a lot of episodes of obsessive-compulsive disorder during my life, and cleanliness had always been one of my big obsessions, so now the OCD took over big-time.

I started ordering people who came through the door to put antibacterial gel on their hands right away. I even raised my voice at one lady who left a tissue next to the bin in the waiting room.

Used tissues are supposed to go *inside* a waste bin – what exactly was the use of leaving them outside? Paranoia ruled now – I didn't dare touch the kettle any more, after so many people had put their hands on it, and Mum was bringing in our very own supply of pristine paper cups.

Ally's future had started to haunt my thoughts. Once they'd got him medically sound in the Victor Horsley ward, he'd have to go into a rehab unit for a long time. In fact, he might have to go into rehab permanently, or some kind of care home, if I couldn't manage him at home. I didn't sleep at all that night: I spent hours researching rehab units on the web.

On Day 30, someone from the Victor Horsley ward came down to ask if Ally was coming up, and our lovely nurse said no, they wanted to keep him for one more day under observation in HD. I was really pleased because I hated the big ward, though of course we were only delaying the inevitable.

Ally was awake a lot, and Dad and I talked to him for most of the day to stimulate him. His speech therapist carried on with his swallowing lessons, giving him four spoonfuls of apple syrup and rubbing his throat as he glugged it down and then coughed a little bit. Ally had a pretty Sikh nurse, who I adored, and she said today was the day: they were taking Ally outside, no matter what. In the end, that was much easier said than done: it took about two hours to get him out into the fresh air.

First they hoisted him into the giant blue chair and bound him in it, and covered him with blankets. Then a man came and wheeled the chair to the lift. Dad and I followed as Ally was taken down and wheeled out to the back of the hospital. This was where he'd come in – it was where the ambulances pulled up with the emergency cases. It was also where some of the patients went for a smoke, so it wasn't exactly the most beautiful or glamorous place for an alfresco excursion. I didn't care, though, because it was the best day of my life so far.

As we stood under a shelter, it poured with rain, and I decided it was the most beautiful rain I'd ever seen. I asked if we could take Ally just outside the shelter so he could feel the rain on his face, but we weren't allowed to do that, because he still had the drain fixed on his head, and it wouldn't do to get that wet. So he couldn't feel the rain because of the drain on his brain... But he was outside, which was cause for celebration.

I phoned Brenda, Mum and Kaz and put the phone to Ally's ear, and he said hello to them, which made Dad and me very emotional.

Back at HD, they were getting ready for Ally's departure to the big ward. They were taking the arterial line out of his groin, and preparing for his brain drain to be removed soon. But his heart was racing — his heart rate was 154 — and I didn't think he was well enough to leave here yet. It had been great to get him outside, but sadly he had no memory of the experience.

He told me today that his favourite food was 'sausages'. Well, I knew for a fact that his favourite food was really sushi, but any word he managed to speak was fine with me. Okay then, Ally, sausages it is.

We hadn't had any bad news for a while, and his trip outside had been wonderful, so it came as a huge shock when we heard the next day that Ally was back in critical. He'd had a major temperature spike during the night and become totally unresponsive. On top of that, he'd had a vasospasm episode, turned grey and passed out. They thought he might have had another stroke. I couldn't believe what I was hearing

Luckily, a scan showed there were no grey wavy lines, so he hadn't had a stroke, and Ally was coming out of critical again. False alarm. Just after he was wheeled back into HD, I had a phone call. Karen had gone into labour. Days before, I'd asked Kaz if she could hold my niece in her belly for a while, at least until I knew that Ally was going to live, and she'd said she would see what she could do.

Now the first baby in the new generation of our little family was about to be born, right on the day that Ally had come back out of critical. It was magical timing. Kaz was only round the corner in the Portland Hospital, a 25-minute walk away. But Ally had his eyes open, and I couldn't bear the idea of him staring into space without me there. I wanted to stay there and stimulate him, so I suggested that Dad go and see Karen now, and I'd go as soon as Ally was having his body turned or washed, or when he fell asleep.

I chatted to Ally, told him everything that was happening, reminded him where he was and what had happened to him, and he said 'Why are you being so cryptic?' before drifting off and going quiet again. I asked him what he was thinking and he returned to me then, replying 'I'm thinking about the word "lop".' I laughed my head off at that bit of nonsense. Around 3pm there was an emergency. It wasn't Ally this time: there'd been a toxic waste spill somewhere on the second floor, all the alarms were going off and we had to evacuate the building. I had to leave Ally and stand in the street while he and a lot of other patients were moved to another, safer place in the hospital. It was a huge worry, because I didn't know where he was now, and whether anyone was keeping watch over him. What if he had another vasospasm episode, or a heart attack?

No matter what I did, I couldn't persuade the people at the front desk, or the firemen who'd arrived to deal with the emergency, to let me back in to see my sick husband. Instead of pacing up and down and panicking outside the hospital, I decided there was only one thing to do.

So I ran round the corner, without my coat or my bag, to see Karen and my new niece, Rose. Rose was gorgeous. Her nose was still a bit squished up and hadn't popped out yet – we have a long tradition of comedy noses in the Poole family – so I call her Rose the Nose. She seemed very calm. I loved her already, and I wished Ally could have seen her. But soon my whole body started to shake, and the urge to get back to the other hospital became overpowering. All I was going to do was sit beside him and try to talk to him, and watch him in all his various states of craziness, but that was simply what I had to do. I couldn't do anything else.

Dad came back with me, and while they washed Ally again, we went for a spot of visualization in the chapel. I pictured Ally still in his hospital bed, wrapped in a blanket, but he was talking to me and answering questions, and he was looking at me properly – not looking right through me as he was really doing. I also imagined us laughing together, but for some reason I found it hard to keep the picture, which kept blurring.

So I switched to trying to slow his heart rate, and concentrated really hard on that, and that was much easier. I pictured us on holiday; he was on a reclining chair, with his chest rising and falling really slowly and calmly as he breathed normally.

In reality, Ally was currently breathing eight or nine breaths to every one of mine – I'd counted. I think it was about an hour later when Dad woke me up – the visualization had blended into a dream. Unfortunately, somehow I was left with a nagging idea that Ally would get better physically but his brain wouldn't. I needed a mental clear-out of some kind, to banish negative thoughts like that.

We raced back to Ally's bed, both feeling we might be missing something. Dad said it was as if we were being drawn back by a magnet, or answering a kind of telepathic summons. Dad can talk for Britain. He'd always been very slow and precise when he spoke, and it would usually drive me mad – 'Yeah yeah, come on, get to the point, Dad!' But his measured approach seemed entirely appropriate now, as he told Ally in laborious detail what had happened to him: he'd had a brain injury and it was a very bad one, and so on and so on... It didn't seem that Ally was with us then, but right out of the blue, his eyes looked straight at Dad and he spoke again.

'How did it happen?' he asked.

Dad was shocked, but he kept his composure and told him the whole story.

'Is it like a stroke?' Ally asked. Wow. Oh my God. These were damned good questions, revealing some serious intelligence and self-awareness. As it was going so well, Dad and I decided to try a test to see how good Ally's memory was. The doctors' theory was that when he was responsive, he was retaining information for a maximum of about four seconds. It was like the old myth of the goldfish in the bowl, swimming round and continually forgetting everything it had seen and done before the past few moments. But, from some of the things Ally had been saying to us, we thought his memory was better than that. So we said, 'Ally, you're in the hospital. That's where you are, in the hospital.' Then we counted up to four, and asked: 'Ally, where are you?'

'I'm in the hospital,' he replied, proving our point.

Dad and I grin at each other – this is real bloody progress, this is. 'Okay, Ally, you're in the hospital... One, two, three four... Do you know where you are, Ally?'

'In the hospital,' he replied again.

We applauded, and I kissed him. Okay, we decided, we'd take this further. 'Ally, this is a hospital. You're in a hospital.' I walked to the end of the bed with Dad, counting out loud: 'One, two, three, four, *five*...' Then I spun round, and with all the hope in the world I asked 'Ally, do you know where you are?'

And, quick as a flash, he replied 'I think I'm somewhere near Norwich.'

Dad and I fell to the floor, laughing. Oh well, at least he hadn't said he was at Wembley Stadium, or on a spaceship. And they do have hospitals near Norwich, you know.

They sealed off his brain drain that night, and that scared me, because the last time they'd done that he was back on life support an hour later. But let's hope for the best, I thought, and see what tomorrow brings.

CHAPTER 16

ON Day 32 I insisted that Dad have another day off, because it was just too stressful for him to spend every single day driving down at 6am, hanging around at the hospital and going back at 10pm. He was nearly 68 years old, for God's sake, and I felt I had to start getting used to dealing with all of this on my own now. Mum said that when Dad was at home, all he did was sit by the phone in a panic, but we both persuaded him to take a day off anyway.

Ally seemed to have regressed – he was immobile again, and couldn't remember his name any more. He'd had another massive temperature spike in the night, and his consultant said it might be that his brain couldn't control his temperature, which was likely to be due to brain damage, because they couldn't find any infections now. Oh no, I didn't like that – find a bloody infection fast, I thought.

The female nurse that Ally had now had been doing some reiki work on him. This wasn't an official NHS service: it was something she practised that had worked for her before. Reiki is an alternative treatment that originated in Japan, and is based on the transfer of healing energy from the hands. Like acupuncturists, reiki practitioners believe that our life force, or chi, flows through the body via a system of meridians. The nurse gave me a photocopy of a meridian chart, so that I could work with important pressure points on Ally's face.

She showed me how to tap an area like the chin or just above an eyebrow to unblock certain meridians and get the energy moving again. She said reiki could be really beneficial for patients with strokes and brain damage, and I hoped it was good for trauma too, because then I could use it on myself as well. I got going with the reiki while Ally was in his big chair, and he gurgled a bit as I applied pressure to points on his face. Unfortunately, he chose this moment to have one of his unexpected attacks.

He tensed and sat upright as the colour visibly drained from him, leaving him looking very grey, and his eyes bulged and rolled back into his head as he slumped over.

'Ally! Ally! Oh my God, Ally!' I shouted, but there was no response. I called for help, and the nurses rushed over and asked me to leave right away. I stood outside the door, terrified but desperate to see what was going on, and I saw three critical nurses dashing in to help him. He looked dead again.

While I was outside the hospital, phoning Dad, I saw Terry Martin (our dear friend and old Alisha's Attic co-songwriter) and his wife Anne arrive. They'd brought their baby Sam, my brand-new godson, who was gorgeous and smiley and seemed to like me. I told Terry that I didn't even know if Ally was alive at this point, and that I'd heard them say he might have had another stroke. I heard myself saying all this so matter-of-factly, it felt like I was having an out-of-body experience. I could well be losing it, I thought – Ally had really taken enough now, and so had I.

The staff let me back in HD after I begged them, and I saw they had Ally in an odd position on the bed, with his head hanging near the floor and his feet in the air. He'd had a big vasospasm episode, they said. He was sleeping for a long time after that, and when the consultants came and tried to wake him, there was no response at all. The brain drain was back, and I could see a lot of scary yellow matter going into the bag. I felt strongly that his latest attack had been inevitable; I didn't think my first attempt at reiki was responsible for it, and in fact I wanted to learn more about this alternative treatment. The nurse explained you could get a special CD that sends out electronic pulses to your meridian lines via an antenna. I decided I could leave that playing when I left at night, so Ally could be mending while he slept. As with the crystals, the visualization and all our appeals to the archangels, I felt there was no harm in trying it, and in fact I wouldn't have forgiven myself if I hadn't tried it. The whole package cost about 150 quid, though, so I decided I wouldn't tell anyone, because they'd think I was mental.

By Saturday, October 10 (Day 33), Ally had outstayed his welcome in HD, and he was moved into the Victor Horsley ward on the second floor, which I'd been dreading. I knew that if he'd been compos mentis at this point, he'd have said: 'Get me out of here, Shell.' He was in a bed down the first aisle, near the door. Seeing him in here now, I suddenly noticed was how noisy the ward was. For so long we'd been used to a subdued environment, with long silences punctuated by quiet conversation and the occasional beeps of machinery, but in this ward there was a TV on and a lot of general chatter from the other patients.

Apart from being hooked up to three machines, having a shaved head and a brain drain attached, Ally looked fairly normal, so the other patients initially tried to involve him in their conversations. He'd contribute a few odd, random remarks, which confused some of the patients until I explained he was brain-damaged.

'Oh, sorry, I didn't realize,' one of them would say, and then continue chatting to the others. At one point I caught myself whispering, to nobody in particular: 'Oh, why are we here?' It was a rhetorical question; I wasn't expecting a reply from anyone. But Ally piped up: 'Because I've had an aneurysm,' which seemed a pretty sensible answer. But he was still fantasizing and confabulating as well.

He told me he'd emailed our friend Connor. 'You didn't, darling – you're in hospital,' I explained. 'Actually, I did,' he argued curtly, to which I responded: 'Where's your computer, then?' And he looked at me in disgust and rolled his eyes as if to say: 'Silly woman!'

He was in that bed for a few days, and he wasn't sleeping well, to the point where they were having to sedate him at night. So they decided the first aisle was too noisy and stimulating for him, and they moved him to the quieter second aisle, among the other patients with brain injuries, who were all quite old and poorly. He was in the last bed by the window – Bed 4 again.

On his first day, his new physio, speech therapist and occupational therapist came to say hello. They all seemed warm, friendly and instantly likeable. They said Ally was the first 'grade 5' they'd dealt with, and they soon started calling him their 'star patient'. I got the feeling he was a bit of a case study for them. All the staff were run ragged with looking after all these patients. They were doing their best, but, as Dr Silverhair had warned, there were so many demands on them that there wasn't enough time in the day to do all the physio that I wanted for Ally. So I asked for lists of things I could do to help. The physio wasn't too much of a problem, though he had no movement from the waist down, so it was hefty work. I'd massage his legs, feet, arms and hands to move his fluids about. For the OT (occupational therapy) we brought in all the pictures that had been around his bed before, as well as books, pens and paper, as he was eventually going to need to read and write again.

I also brought in his music, his camera and his computer – maybe he would really be emailing again soon, rather than just dreaming about doing it. I brought in some of his clothes from home, as well. I thought I was jumping the gun a bit on some of this, but I thought he might feel more normal and human and click into some kind of spontaneous behaviour when he saw his things there.

For speech therapy, all we could do was ask him questions and yak away and hope he'd join in, like we'd been doing for weeks. He was speaking a lot now, but so much of what he said didn't make sense; in fact, sometimes it was so random and irrational that it was quite scary. Once, he was staring intently at the poor man opposite, and when I asked why, he said: 'We've been discussing cheating at cards, and he told me to throw them under the car and run them over – then I'll win!' Talking about the same man, he told me: 'All he thinks of is sandwiches, and they give him two biscuits and I only get one, but it's fluorescent, so it's okay.'

One day Ally looked particularly sad in his bed, and I asked what was up. 'I can't pull things out of the air any more,' he replied. 'What, like words?' I asked, thinking he was being metaphorical, and he said: 'No, like things I can touch – shapes... wire...' It seemed like I was spending all my time correcting him, saying: 'No, babe, that didn't happen,' and making him cross all the time. The experts said that I shouldn't correct him if it makes him unhappy, but how could he learn the difference between reality and fantasy if we didn't address it? I didn't want him to carry on living in Cloud Cuckoo Land, so for his own good I decided I'd be the bad guy for a while and correct him. If he hated me for doing that, he'd just have to hate me until he was finally in his right mind. Some of the things he was saying were quite nasty, shocking and totally out of character, and made me worry about the things I'd read about personality changes. Seeing a celebrity in a magazine, he declared: 'I want to kick them to death!'

He could be hurtful too. Once, he said there was 'a pain in front of my phone', so I jumped up helpfully and sai:d 'What can I do? Where, babe?' And he said 'What part do you not understand about that, stupid cow?'

But he could also be hysterically funny. On his first night in the Victor Horsley ward, I asked him what he would most like to eat, and he licked his lips and said: 'Griddled purée,' and looked very confused when I laughed. He told me that our wallpaper at home had 'carrots' on it, and, looking at a picture of little Rose, he declared that she looked like 'a toe'. When a nurse dropped a tray nearby, he said 'Ooh, sounds like a Japanese accident – small and delicate.' Perhaps most embarrassing of all was the moment when his consultant came to see about removing his brain drain. While she was leaning right over him and looking at the drain, I asked why his heart rate was still so high, and she replied: 'I think he's probably got fibrillated arteries.' Immediately, Ally, mimicking her voice, said the word 'farteries' right in her face. I didn't know where to look.

He was also starting to move his hands more now, but unfortunately they stayed mostly around his genitals. He would get his bits out all the time and show them to anybody and everybody. When I tried to pretend it wasn't happening and discreetly moved his hands away, he'd laugh, tut or give me an exasperated look and just carry on. When his visitors left (Mum, Dad, Steve, Holly, Paul, Sandra, Terry, Anne, Charity, cousin Kerry, Adam – they were all lucky enough to be part of this wonderful time) I'd tell him off and ask him how he'd feel if I got my boobs out in front of his friends, but he just found that hysterical as well. It frightened me to think that this lack of inhibitions could have been down to those frontal-lobe strokes.

He was being naughty in other ways too. He could move his right arm jerkily up to his head now, and he kept trying to remove his brain drain, even though I continually explained what it was and told him not to. He was also risking serious infections by putting his hands everywhere and then touching his head. And they'd told me that if he got another infection now, it was straight back into bloody critical.

They ended up binding his hands and putting these padded white gloves on them, which looked like boxing gloves. The gloves killed two birds with one stone, because he'd been pulling his feeding tube out of his nose as well.

As Mum and I were getting ready to say goodbye to him one night, I saw he was trying to bite off the plaster stuck round the wrist of one of the gloves, so he could get it off. He was looking at me with such yearning, pleading with me silently to help him. 'I can't, Ally,' I told him, 'because you'll just touch your head and pull your tube out.'

'No I won't,' he said, shaking his head. 'Just do it and it'll be our secret.'

Mum, who's usually a stickler for rules, was on his side. 'Oh, take them off, Shell – he's so frustrated,' she said. I explained that this happened every day, and that I knew full well what he was going to do.

'No, I think he'll be okay this time,' she said. And she asked Ally to promise he wouldn't pull out the tube.

'I promise, Pam,' he said – before she took the gloves off for him. 'Don't let me down, Ally,' she said.

'I won't, Pam,' he replied. She gave him a kiss and left. I walked her to the lift, and by the time I'd returned to the bed he'd pulled the bloody tube out!

Every night before I left, I'd put the reiki CD on and leave it with the antenna on the bedside cabinet, about a metre away from his head. I'd stick a really nice photograph of us, in which we were both smiling, on his bed with Blu-Tack so he'd wake up to it. And I'd get busy with some Post-it notes, writing messages to tell the night nurses not to move the CD, and scribbling little reminders for Ally as well. I'd write something like 'I've gone home to Muswell Hill. You're still in the hospital. I'll be back in the morning at 9. Look at the clock to your left, so you know the time,' and I'd stick the note on the bed where he could see it. And I'd write another one saying: 'Don't pull your tube out of your nose. It's your food and you hate having it put back in, remember!'

I'd seen them put the tube back in once, and it was a horrible procedure: Ally thrashed around and tried to fight the nurses off, and they held him down and pushed the tube up his nose and all the way to his stomach. He could pull it out in a flash, but it could take them two hours to put it back.

If only he could retain the vaguest memory of how awful that was, he would have left that tube well alone!

CHAPTER 17

THE official opening time for visitors in the Victor Horsley ward was 10am, but I'd broken the rules. I'd cried my eyes out in front of the head nurse one day, complaining that I couldn't simply sit in my empty house and wait for an extra hour every morning to see Ally. So now I usually got there at 8.45, just after they did the ward rounds. I'd also suggested I take some of Ally's burden off them – I could change him, wash him, get him to clean his teeth and give him breakfast. I'd learnt how to change the sheets without having to hoist him out of bed, though it involved a complicated series of manoeuvres and took about 40 minutes. I was allowed now to go into the cupboards where they kept the fresh linen and bedpans, though I'd never asked – I just did it one day and they'd got used to it.

Today, Day 35, they had him in a groovy new wheelchair, though he wasn't strong enough to sit in it properly and he had no sense of balance, so he was slumping to the left side of it.

They told him to try to line himself up with something straight, like a door or window, but he couldn't get that and just laughed. He was so uncomfortable sitting in the wheelchair, and he was unable to shift his body to make it any better. They wanted him to start using his arms to propel himself along in the chair, but that just wasn't going to happen yet. I gave him some apple syrup to help him practise swallowing, massaging his throat just under his Adam's apple to help him.

Weirdly, this was fun, and we both started grinning about it. Then he tried to get me in a headlock, and we burst out laughing. I saw him try to pull the feeding tube out yet again, so I put the boxing gloves back on him and stuck the plaster around his wrists. We tried some boxing physio after that, with me putting my hands up to see how hard he could punch them. It took his mind off the gloves for five seconds, but then he wanted to bite them off again.

The staff were concerned that his heart rate was 148 beats per minute today – that's nearly 2½ beats per second! The average man should have a heart rate of something like 60 to

80. They'd put him on 'cardiac watch' because of that, and we had a big red button by the bed to remind us that his life was hanging in the balance again.

Ward visitors had to leave promptly at 1pm to give the patients an hour's 'sleep time', and I hated that: it was so arbitrary, and didn't make sense because he was still sleeping for most of the day anyway. Also, I wanted to be here if he woke up and needed something. Lately he'd been getting confused and doing destructive things, like opening the valve on his catheter bag so that his pee went everywhere; then he couldn't move himself or communicate to anyone, so he was just lying in pee until someone happened to notice. So every day at 1pm there was an argument about me wanting to stay but having to leave, which I never won.

Today he actually remembered some information from the other day – that he'd said little Rose looked like 'a toe'. He was also doing pretty well in the toe department himself: at one point, as he was being observed, he wiggled one of his toes on command before our very eyes. He also succeeded in pushing his foot down into the nurse's hand; it was quite a weak effort, but it was an achievement.

Some days were a lot of fun. I was laughing a lot with him, though his laughter was soundless at the moment. Also, his friends were coming to see him so frequently that it was like he was having a party – Mum, Dad, Paul, Sandra, Dave and Steve had barely missed a day. But the nurses said they'd have preferred him to be less happy, which sounded cruel until they explained that when a patient started to get really frustrated and wanted to leave, it was a good sign that they were getting better.

It wasn't a good sign that whenever Ally was hoisted back into bed, he'd exclaim: 'Ooooh, home!'

I thought if I started doing some proper physio with him now, he'd build up some strength and start wanting to get out of his bedridden state. So I roped in some of our friends and we all got to work. Being strong, Terry and Paul could do the big, hefty stuff. We made him arm-wrestle, and also got him to push our bodies away with his legs.

ut it had become clear that he couldn't remember how to follow instructions and do the simplest tasks. He was getting 'push' and 'pull' mixed up, he couldn't tell his left arm or leg from his right, and he was unable to throw a ball because he couldn't let go of it.

He tried to throw and ended up staring at the ball as if to say: 'Why can't I let go of this? What's going on?'

Getting him to brush his own teeth was interesting. I'd lay all the equipment out on a table for him, as the occupational therapist had suggested – his toothbrush, toothpaste, a bowl of water and a paper towel. I'd pause to see if he could initiate the brushing procedure, but he never could, so I'd have to prompt him: 'Right, Ally, you're going to clean your teeth. What do you need to do first?' And he'd look like a helpless child then, staring down at the equipment and then up at me with a confused expression.

'Okay,' I'd say, 'you need to pick up your toothbrush and put some toothpaste on it.' He'd nod knowingly then, as if to say

'Of course!' But then, disappointingly, he'd pick up the paper towel and put it between his lips.

'No, that's not quite right, hon. Let's take that out and try again.' Then he'd just repeat the paper-towel trick again, while looking confused and gazing intently at his hand and the toothbrush. Somewhere the wires were getting crossed: it was as if he knew exactly what to do and in what order to do it in, but he just couldn't get his hand to do what he wanted. It was like his inability to tell the difference between 'push' and 'pull', and 'do' and 'don't' – 'Ally, *don't* turn that valve. That'll just cover the bed in… Right, I'll go and get fresh sheets…'

By Day 39, his arms and legs seemed to be doing so well, they tried to get him to stand in a special supporting frame. It was a great big contraption that he was fastened into with a belt, and the idea was that it would lift him electronically into a standing position.

Unfortunately, he had a vasospasm episode right at that moment and passed out. Ally was hard work in all kinds of ways.

One day he was in his wheelchair and I was giving him the usual 'You're in the hospital' routine, when he said 'You see that guy in the end bed? He's my grandad, John Weir. He fought in Vietnam.'

Now, Ally's grandad John Weir really did fight in Vietnam, but the guy in the end bed was a stranger, just another patient here, and I told him so. He didn't take it well. 'What are you talking about, Shelly? He is! You don't even know him,' he said. No, no, no, this was a hospital in London, I reminded him. How could John, who had passed away years ago, be here today in the brain unit of a hospital in London? To which Ally replied: 'Because of the war. It's a spy thing.'

I told him patiently that it was impossible, it couldn't be his grandad, and that he was going to have to take my word for it. And he looked at me and replied, with some venom: 'You're going to have to give me more proof! How can I take your word for it?' Okay, he'd asked for it. So I got behind his chair, wheeled him all the way up to the old guy in the end bed – who was actually Chinese, looked quite poorly and was probably blissfully unaware of all this fuss. And I said: 'Because he's fucking Chinese! There! Is that enough proof?'

I'd become the focus for most of Ally's aggression and anger. I'd previously thought that at this stage, I'd be surfing the clouds: he was alive, breathing by himself and getting better day by day. But I'd also been told by the experts that rehabilitation was the hardest part for the patient's carer, and they were so right about that. I still wasn't eating, I was down to seven stone, I'd done my back in and hurt my left arm just trying to lift him, and I was getting no thanks at all from him. And I'd ask myself over and over again: 'Why am I killing myself doing everything for him when he totally hates me for it?' It would have been so easy for me to lose it and break down emotionally when he was being so mean while I was doing my best to be caring and sympathetic, and I had to be careful and retain my self-control. I had to be hard and take no rubbish from him: if he didn't start helping himself now, he'd never get better – he'd be this vegetable for the rest of his life – and that simply wasn't an option.

Though he was being nasty to me, he was perfectly pleasant to all his other visitors. But I took that as a good sign: maybe his inhibitions weren't all gone, because he still wanted to show his good side to most people. But the fantasies raged on. At one point, instead of believing he was in space, in a departure lounge or somewhere near Norwich, he'd decided he was in Big Brother. He was convinced that he was in a gigantic studio, all the nurses were actors, and everything he was doing was going out live on TV. This was ironic because in real life he'd always hated reality shows; they made his blood boil. But now, if I said something like: 'We must get your tracksuit bottoms on before Paul gets here,' he'd reply: 'There's no point, Shell – they've seen it all anyway. We can't hide anything in here.'

Talking about a member of staff who'd come to see him recently, he said 'That nurse earlier is a famous actor. I think he's here to try and baffle me, but I know who he is. It's all just for telly, eh!' I was getting tired of the Big Brother routine by now, so I called the nurse over and asked him to explain that he wasn't an actor, and that Ally was in a real hospital. But Ally just gave a knowing smile and said: 'It's okay – I'm in on it.' When I made him look in a mirror to show him proof of the surgery he'd had on his head, he panicked and called out really loudly to the head nurse, and as she ran over he cried: 'Nurse, help! This woman is trying to mislead me!'

On Day 41, Ally had been sitting for a long time in his big chair, and it was starting to hurt him so much that he was crying and turning a funny colour. But the nurses were so busy, I couldn't find one to get him back to bed. I massaged his legs in an effort to ease the pain, and he had a real go at me. 'You're more worried about things being tidy than how uncomfortable I am,' he told me. I turned my back when I started crying, so he didn't see the tears.

He was miles away for the rest of the day, and I laid my head on his chest for about two hours. I left the hospital feeling totally knackered and upset. And when I returned on Day 43, I heard he hadn't slept that night. Not only that, but he'd pulled the feeding tube half out, which resulted in fluid going down into his lungs. They were trying to put the tube back in, but they couldn't be sure where it was now, whether it was in his stomach or his lungs, so they had to give him another scan. Later that day, his therapists and I got him to write his name and address: it didn't look good, and the concentration exhausted him.

But he did make some real progress with his orientation. For a long time he'd seemed to be stuck in the year 1986 – which would have made him 17 or 18 years old – but now he knew it was 2009, and he remembered he was in a hospital. He'd left the reality-TV show now, which was good.

A consultant came to see how he was doing, and she asked him to move his left leg – and he did. 'What do you want me to do now?' he asked her afterwards, rather cheekily.

He was definitely getting stronger now, and I got him to practise pushing my shoulder with his foot and to do three high-fives – and I made sure they were really high. I laid my head on his chest again, and this time he lowered one of his gloved hands onto my hair, which felt like a cuddle.

Unfortunately, he showed his penis to everyone again today, and I was embarrassed when the nurses requested that we kept him covered up when visitors came in to see the other patients.

Our friend John Richmond, the fashion designer, came to see him, and Ally sat in his chair and communicated with us for three hours. I asked all his visitors to try not to laugh if Ally said anything strange, because it seemed cruel to laugh at him, and laughter wasn't an appropriate reaction to the serious condition he was in. And John and I tried our best not to laugh, but then the nurse casually asked Ally what he'd been up to lately, and he replied: 'I've been trampolining with the Russian president.' That was so hilarious that we couldn't help ourselves, and we just cracked up.

CHAPTER 18

ONE day I was minding my own business in the Victor Horsley ward, trying to teach Ally how to use the emergency call button for the nurses if he needed help, when the head staff nurse dragged a chair up and sat down next to me. He was clutching a sheaf of paperwork and looked like a man on a mission, and I could feel an argument brewing.

Shelly, you know that Ally has to go into a rehab unit,' he reminded me. 'We need the bed now, and we can't really do any more for him here. Ally is a grade 5, so his brain is very poorly and he needs very specialist help, both physically and mentally.' He told me Ally would be going to live in a unit for at least nine months, maybe a whole year, and that an application had been made for a place at Homerton Hospital in Hackney, east London – and Ally had been accepted. He handed the documents to me, and I read that Homerton's RNRU (Regional Neurological Rehabilitation Unit) specialized in inpatient rehab for young adult patients who'd experienced certain 'neurological events'. Visitors could come and see him there between 4pm and 8pm.

I was in tears. I'd known that this would be coming, that we'd have to leave this place at some point, but the staff knew Ally so well here and we felt so safe here, and it all seemed so sudden and so sad. And I hated the idea of putting him in Hackney and not seeing him until 4pm every day for nine whole months. Couldn't he go into the intense rehab unit in this hospital, I asked the head nurse – that looked great, it was just upstairs, and he'd only be there for 12 weeks.

'I'm afraid Ally is nowhere near the physical and mental level you need to be at for intense rehab,' he explained. 'He needs to be able to concentrate on one task for at least half an hour, and he can't do more than five minutes.'

Then he shocked me by saying that I mustn't make this 'all about me' – I should be thinking about what's best for my husband. I had to restrain myself from being very unladylike and putting my fist in his face, and we had a proper row instead.

'How dare you!' I said. 'It's all about Ally. I know him, and he won't stay there. And you say he's not at that level? Well, I work with him every day, and he concentrates for a lot longer than you say he does. He's using humour, he's moving his legs and feet... I think you've assessed him wrongly.'

We battled for at least 15 minutes, and I realized the cold truth — that we were just one of countless problems in this man's working day. So I gave in, at least for the time being.

The nurse said they thought the RNRU was the very best option for Ally, and anything else might be 'detrimental to his progress'. But although Ally had to leave this hospital, his bed at the RNRU wasn't available yet. So he'd have to go to the Royal Free Hospital in Hampstead for two weeks in the meantime.

I phoned Dad and told him the news. He was at the other hospital round the corner, visiting Rose, and he and Dave jumped straight into the car and drove to Hackney to check out Ally's prospective new home. They got to the main door of Homerton Hospital and didn't like the look of the area at all, and they decided there and then: no, absolutely not, no way could he come here. But they were just about to get back in the car when Dave suggested, as they were there anyway, they take a look inside the rehab unit itself. And they found it was nice, clean and spacious, and the patients were doing some painting and making baskets, and Dad and Dave said, well, this isn't so bad. But it was in quite a scary area, and I'd have to take the car. Basket-making? 'Ally would hate that,' I said. The information the head nurse had given me said that 'lots of group activity is encouraged'. Ugh, he'd hate that too. And he'd only get three guaranteed physio sessions a week, so what would he be doing for the rest of the time? Sitting in bed, staring into the distance – that's what. It occurred to me that 'rehab' like this was exactly the kind of thing that would be 'detrimental to his progress'. So we had a fight on our hands.

When I asked Ally what sort of rehab he'd prefer – intense and fast, or nice and slow – I was getting mixed answers. But I got a great email back from Edwyn Collins's wife, Grace, advising us to go for the rehab unit we wanted and not to take no for an answer. Dad said something similar – go with your gut instinct and don't let anyone sway you, he advised. He said if I thought Ally was well enough to go into intense rehab, then he probably was – I was the one who saw him every day and knew exactly what progress he was making.

So I went back to the head nurse and told him I'd given it a lot of thought, and unless we could get an assessment for the rehab unit upstairs, I'd be signing him out of the hospital today, and I'd be taking him home and doing all his rehab myself. Could we have an ambulance now, please?

Of course, it was a ludicrous idea for him to leave today for home rehab. But I was determined that he wouldn't go to the Homerton – it was upstairs or nothing. I won the battle: that day, they booked an assessment for the rehab unit here, for five days' time.

Aware that we suddenly had a lot of work to do, I spoke to his occupational therapist and speech therapist, who were really supportive and said they'd do absolutely everything in their power to ensure he was ready for that assessment. I knew they would, too, because these people had already worked wonders. We'd been in this ward for 18 days, and in that time Ally had come along in leaps and bounds. His limbs were moving, he was standing in a frame for up to five minutes at a time, and we could take him outside in his wheelchair. He could write his name, clean his teeth (he'd stopped doing the stupid paper-towel trick), hold his camera, laugh and tell jokes. He was slowly becoming normal in other ways.

I'd dressed him in some of his own clothes, which wasn't easy because he couldn't lift his bum at all, and I'd shown him his reflection in the mirror to give him a better idea of who he was. After I did that, I often found him staring at his own reflection, coming to terms with the man in the mirror.

At least three times a week I'd take him out and push him around Soho in his wheelchair, and I'd stop occasionally to show him his reflection in a shop window. But I think the main thing that moved him forward at this point was regaining his ability to swallow. He'd been made to practise a lot with apple syrup and was doing really well, and one afternoon they said they'd decided not to use the feeding tube any more, and to start him on a puréed-food diet.

It was exciting news, the beginning of him feeding himself properly again, and Sandra and I raced to Waitrose in the Brunswick Centre and bought all kinds of yoghurts and creamy desserts – they said full-fat cream was very good for brain injuries. We also got him a takeaway coffee and a bag of Quavers – okay, they're not puréed food exactly, but they do dissolve on the tongue.

Ally ate and drank all these new delights, and while he didn't quite understand our joy and excitement at seeing him do that, he totally loved it. His face was a picture of happiness, and ours were too.

One day, we were given some shocking inside information. Ally and I were with Connor and Louisa in the chapel, where we'd often go to hang out and play the organ or the piano. As we were messing about on the gigantic organ, in rushed a nurse I knew from the critical-care ward, where Ally had spent so much of his life when he'd first come to the hospital. She'd glimpsed Ally in here through the window, and was so pleasantly surprised that he was up and about and doing so well now. 'It's a miracle!' she said.

Now he was better, she said, she could tell us the truth about Bed 4, where Ally had spent his first 29 days at this hospital. In the many years she'd worked here, not one patient had lived after being put in that bed, and all the staff called it Dead Space for that reason. And when she'd seen me with Ally there on our first day, she'd gone to the head nurse and said 'Get that young couple out of Dead Space now – they're too young!' She said she'd seen me bending over Ally and laughing and singing to him when he was in his coma, and she'd thought we looked too alive for that bed. The head nurse had said no, he was a 'grade 5 subarachnoid' and they couldn't move him. But now she was thrilled that he'd come out of there alive; she said we'd broken Bed 4's chain of bad luck. The story gave me shivers down my spine – at the time, we'd thought we had the best spot in the house, in the corner right by the window – in Dead Space!

After I'd been living alone in my quiet and empty house for weeks, My oldest friend, the artist Adam Regester, came to stay for a while. He'd moved to Spain eight years before and I missed him a lot, so it was great to see him, and he was able to help me with the daily hospital grind. Adam and I would do some good physio with Ally: we'd take one of his legs each and move it round in a circle, and we'd try to improve the circulation in his toes.

By this time, there were quite a few other old friends and colleagues of Ally's who were eager to visit him, and I'd been asking him if he wanted to see them. One minute he'd say: 'Oh, that'd be lovely,' and the next it would be: 'Oh no!'

I decided to wait a bit, until he was properly settled in the ward and ready to face everyone, before I invited more visitors here.

Seeing more people would be good for his memory, and maybe it would help him learn to behave with some restraint, rather than making inappropriate comments, getting naked all the time and showing his bits!

So, after a month-and-a-half of receiving text updates on Ally's condition, his old Texas bandmates started coming in – Sharleen Spiteri, Johnny McElhone, Michael Bannister and their managers, Rab and Gerry. I was still concerned that Ally might find it stressful seeing someone from his working life, and before Sharleen arrived at the hospital on October 25 (day 48), Ally hadn't seen her for a few years.

Texas were the kind of band who regrouped every now and then for an album and a tour, and they hadn't done much together since 2005. But he engaged well with her – so well that he even asked if she wouldn't mind getting him some fish and chips. Can you believe the cheek: he hadn't seen here in years, and now he was asking his famous lead singer to fetch him some fish and chips!

Anyway, Sharleen was fine about it and sourced the very best fish and chips and came back at 6pm. She was all dressed up to go out, but she made a point of attending to Ally's wishes first, which was really sweet of her.

During Ally's time in this ward, his Texas friends didn't restrict themselves to delivering fish-and-chip takeaways: they also brought him some Celtic memorabilia, which he was thrilled with, and all manner of other things from Scotland: Scottish newspapers, Irn-Bru, and sweets you couldn't buy in England. Ally was having a problem with dry skin and eczema, so Sharleen brought in an amazing skin cream, which literally cleared it up within 24 hours. They'd push him round in his wheelchair on the lovely little green opposite the hospital, and they'd all chat with him and get him to join in their banter.

On the same day as Sharleen's first visit, Paul, Sandra, Connor, Louisa and I took Ally down to the chapel to see if he fancied playing a spot of piano. He did some tinkling with one finger, but it was uncomfortable for him to keep his arm up for a long time, so I ended up joking that his piano-playing had always been rubbish anyway! It was like that old joke about the injured hospital patient who says: 'Doctor, will I be able to play the violin when I'm better?' And the doc says 'Absolutely, no problem,' to which the patient replies 'That's wonderful – I could never play it before!'

I'd suggested the staff take his catheter out today, and they did it on the condition that I go on urine watch, making sure that he peed in a bottle rather than in his bed. It was something he still needed to get the hang of: I was on his case all day, and they had to change his bed at least seven times. But I was convinced we'd get there eventually. And now he was completely free of tubes – I had a tube-free husband! Ally came out with some proper mad shit that day.

'Get me shoes, Shell,' he announced once, 'and I'll run you home in the car.' And he told me he couldn't come out with me in his wheelchair today, because he'd been put in charge of something very important, involving the man in the next bed. Unfortunately, he couldn't remember what this top-priority assignment was exactly. 'I think I have to count his sandwiches,' he revealed earnestly after a while.

October 27 was a very important day. As well as being Day 50 of this whole nightmare, this was the day when Ally would be assessed for the intense-rehab unit at the hospital. He was awake when I arrived at the ward – and naked. The nurse explained that lately he'd been stripping off every night. How embarrassing!

After he was properly covered up, a stern lady came to give him the first assessment, and I asked to sit in. 'Where are you?' she asked him, along with 'Which toe am I touching?' Then she asked him to lift his right hand and bring it up to his head. I thought he'd done well, apart from having no idea which toe it was, or what was left or right. The stern lady left, giving nothing away, and I was so nervous.

Ally had a lot of stimulating therapy on his big day. First they spruced him up and put him in his wheelchair, and he did some writing in his diary with the help of his speech therapist. Then his occupational therapist took him for his first bathroom shave – up to this point, he'd shaved in bed. She made him look at his reflection to see how he was sitting, and tried to get him to improve his posture. Then they tried something really ambitious: to get him to stand without using the big machine. It took four women and an enormous collective effort (his occupational therapist was very nearly squashed under him) and it didn't last long, but it was an important step forward. We tried to get him to do some drawing then, but he couldn't concentrate and became bored very quickly.

He was having another assessment in the afternoon, and he needed to have a sleep before that. And he was usually as mad as a brush when he woke up, so he really needed an hour's waking time as well – he was generally quite lucid after an hour. He was out like a light, and unfortunately, despite my attempts to wake him up, he only came to at 3.15pm – just as five female rehab-unit assessors turned up! He'd been asked many questions before by consultants and given stupid answers. 'What's your biggest problem at the moment?' was a common one, and he'd say something random like: 'I can't open the window' or 'I can't spell the word "hyena".' So his therapists and I had been priming him for that question: we told him that when someone asked that question he should say 'I can't walk' – which was a genuine big problem. And now the moment was upon us...

'Ally,' said one of the assessors, 'what do you think your biggest problem is at the moment?' 'Maps!' replied Ally. 'I can't read maps.' Ohhhh, shit. The assessors looked at me and smiled. 'Is there anything else, physically, that's a problem right now, Ally,' one of them asked. 'Yes,' he said, 'I get a little cold at nights.' Oh, bugger. I knew I wasn't supposed to, but I couldn't help butting in to help him. 'Don't you think **walking** is a problem, hon?' 'Oh, yes, of course,' he replied. 'They hide my shoes so I can't walk.' I wanted to curl up and die. But as the assessment continued, Ally became more lucid and cracked some jokes (intentional ones) and they seemed to warm to him. The test ended with one of them asking him if he could manage to go to the loo by himself. With half a dozen women round his bed, Ally was deeply embarrassed at the question. 'Of course I can,' he said. But when they started manipulating his legs to assess how much movement and strength he had, it was obvious that he'd recently wet himself. Could it get worse?

Ally's therapists had a meeting with the five ladies, who then returned to the bed and told me it was 'highly unusual' a person in Ally's condition was able to use humour the way he did – it was quite a 'high-level cognitive response'. And on the basis I'd expressed a desire to keep him at this hospital, they said they'd like to offer him a bed in the intense rehab unit upstairs. He was only bloody well in! I gave his therapists a massive hug each and did a bit of leaping around for joy. I was so happy, I almost started singing, which was what I used to do for a living. We ended that day by listening to a CD by Ricky Gervais, which our friend Holly had brought in for Ally. He ate some plums and laughed his head off, and I was sure I'd never, ever, felt so light and happy before.

CHAPTER 19

I TOLD Pauline that we were working well on Ally's body, we had that covered, but we needed to mend his brain. So the healing circle started to work seriously hard on that. Pauline would text to say what they'd done – how they'd used my earlier idea of visualizing his brain as a filing cabinet, with stacks of paper being put back one at a time.

Then I'd try the same visualization again as well. Ally's own brain knew it needed fixing. I knew that because one day I had him practising some handclaps to improve his coordination, and when I asked him if he could clap three times he said: 'Actually, no – I'm trying to work on my brain at the moment, so I won't. I'll do that first.'

I was stunned to see he had such self-awareness – that he knew about the brain damage and was actually trying to repair it himself.

Pauline said the healing circle had been working on his memory: they'd spent a lot of time imagining Ally recalling situations in which he was playing guitar, playing football or looking at me adoringly on our wedding day. His memory certainly needed a lot of help.

At one point he forgot he couldn't stand and walk, and he got out of bed and had quite a bad fall. It took five strong people to pick him up off the floor. But I thought it was a good sign: it showed he had the motivation to start walking again.

October 31 was his 41st birthday, and his parents came back down from Glasgow with his brother Ross. He had a whole conveyor belt of friends coming in to see him that day as well, and he stayed awake for a long time to greet them all. Dougie was down from Glasgow, and had a football signed by the Celtic team for him (as a Rangers fan, Dougie must have loved him an awful lot to do that). The nurses got him a lovely lemon cake, and we all sang 'Happy Birthday' to him and made him blow out the candles – which was another skill he had yet to remaster properly.

After all the fuss I made about him moving to the Victor Horsley ward, it was actually a sad day when we left the place.

It already felt like home – I'd become totally institutionalized, just as Ally had – and I knew I'd miss his wonderful therapists.

I'd been a few times with Sandra to have a good look at the rehab unit. It had a huge gym and all the latest equipment, and he had a team of really nice ladies I thought he'd respond well to. Ally was waiting in his wheelchair for a porter to take him to the unit, and beside him was another wheelchair stacked with all his medical notes, which were going to the unit with him. The pile of papers nearly reached the ceiling: he'd had one of the longest stays they'd known in the critical-care unit and in this ward too, and I pitied the people who were going to have to look through that lot.

We'd had a talk with the rehab team, and discussed what goals would be desirable and achievable for Ally – including walking, reading, playing guitar and taking photographs. Ally asked to include driving as well. They asked how long we thought it would take, realistically, to achieve those goals, given that we had 12 weeks maximum. I thought nine weeks was realistic, but they said they thought it might take the full 12 weeks. Ally was much more optimistic, saying he could do it in two weeks!

Ally's bed was the one nearest the door in Room 3. The other patients were all staring into the middle distance, and it felt like a scene from One Flew Over the Cuckoo's Nest. They didn't want people to get too comfortable here – the idea was that patients should be encouraged to want to go home – so you weren't allowed to stay in bed all day, or to eat in bed. And there were no nurses as such: only wardens who administered the drugs and cleaned you up.

The first week was assessment week, and after that Ally was given a calendar with all his daily lessons marked on it. Ally was personally responsible for ensuring he got to those lessons on time – they wouldn't come and fetch him if he didn't. He'd have to sound the help buzzer, ask for a warden and a banana board – a plank of wood enabling him to slide from his bed into his wheelchair – and then wheel himself to the gym or the appropriate study room. I thought this would be a disaster: he hadn't a clue what time of day it was, I was sure he'd keep forgetting to look at the calendar, and when he tried to wheel himself along he'd go round in circles, because one of his arms was much stronger than the other. He couldn't even remember to eat and drink without being reminded. I knew when he was getting thirsty, because he'd start getting all antsy and confused until I gave him some water, and then he was fine again. I knew when he wanted to go to the loo because he'd say something odd like: 'I've got to wheel a Tonka truck to Devon.' It was like his own funny personal code, but it was different every time.

I began to worry that we shouldn't really be here, that I shouldn't have pushed for intensive rehab, because none of the other patients appeared to have any major brain damage. I'd watch him gazing into the distance with a glazed expression and I'd think: 'Oh no, what have I done?'

But he instantly made friends with a guy called Tony in the next bed, who'd had a major stroke which had affected the left side of his body. Tony was funny and I liked him a lot, but he kept moaning about the physiotherapists, saying they were rubbish and they didn't do what they said they'd do; worse, he told Ally he should try to escape! I didn't think Tony realized just how impressionable Ally was right now, and Ally was already starting to say some negative things that were really out of character. In fact, I was beginning to notice some changes in his personality, which I found deeply disturbing.

Ally and Tony could be a right pair of old moaners, so I did my best to keep them on happy subjects, which was virtually impossible. Fortunately, Ally was also getting on well with a guy called Cliff, in the bed opposite his. Cliff was 38 and he'd had multiple sclerosis for half his life, since he was 19, but he was so positive and was always laughing and cracking jokes. I was glad he was in Ally's room.

Tony and Cliff tried to include Ally in their conversations, but sometimes they couldn't understand his responses, and he could come across as rude when he didn't reply at all and just stared at them, or when he talked over them. I explained quietly that while he looked fairly normal, he was severely brain-damaged, and they both said they'd look out for him.

Assessment week was tough going. I watched as Ally was asked to do a lot of cognitive tests, like: 'Put all the blue items in a pile, then all the yellow items... Now pile them by shape.' They'd put four things out on the table, take one away and see if Ally could remember what it was. And they'd tell him a little story – Mr Smith was a baker who worked every day in his shop in Glasgow – and then tested his comprehension: what was Mr Smith's occupation, where did he work, and so on?

They asked him to name as many animals as he could in one minute, and he came up with three: caribou, moose and possum. I thought that was amazing, but most people start with the obvious ones like 'cat' and 'dog', which he'd failed to mention. He was also having trouble with putting things in the right order. There was a sequence of cards that showed a watering can, a watering can under a tap, a lady watering plants and then the plants growing – which was obviously the right order – but Ally put the cards in the wrong places. He clearly wasn't quite ready to start gardening again. The tests revealed that he had little if any short-term memory, and he had a problem with his executive skills – he was unable to initiate and stop actions, change his behaviour when a task required him to do so.

His psychologist said that the frontal lobes play a major role in executive skills. But I wasn't too worried about his executive skills, because I wasn't sure they'd been that great in the first place. He'd always been a creative person rather than a practical person. When he'd done certain practical things at home, like following a step-by-step guide to assemble furniture, he'd usually discarded the instructions and done his own thing (and asked me to come and put it right afterwards, usually).

That whole week of mental, physical and medical assessments was knackering for him. He hadn't been awake for such long periods since he'd had the haemorrhage, and ironically he became too tired to put himself to bed, so I had to tuck him in every night. And he kept trying to get up and falling forward onto the floor. He was supposed to pee in a bottle next to his bed, and we'd put all these Post-it notes around the bottle to remind him, but one night he got up and tried to go to the loo instead, and he ended up slipping and somehow landing with his lower body right under his bed, and his head poking out. He'd stayed there for three hours, not knowing what to do.

Cliff and Tony thought it was hysterical, and the four of us spent many an hour laughing and making light of Ally's misadventures. But I was seriously worried about what predicament he'd get himself into next. For so long I'd been looking forward to Ally coming home where he belonged and returning to his normal self, but lately I'd found him difficult company. I told Ally's psychologist about the changes I'd noticed in my husband's personality – I didn't feel that I knew him properly any more – and asked if she thought he'd return to normal. She thought not – we'd have to adapt to cope with the man he was now, she said, which sounded terrifying.

They still wanted him to stay here for the full 12 weeks, but they said by week 10 or 11 he might be able to do a home visit, and he should be ready to come home properly by

February 12. They warned that coming home after being institutionalized for so long would be a stressful business, and suggested I see a psychologist and a social worker to help with all that.

I never would have thought we'd need a social worker in our lives. I hated the idea of that, and felt I was perfectly capable of dealing with everything myself. But I accepted the rehab team's advice and tried to banish my prejudices, and I found the social worker was actually a very nice lady. However, I turned down the offer of a psychologist: I just felt I didn't have the time for that when I was devoting so much of the day to being Ally's carer. The wardens had put Ally on 24-hour watch because he kept falling over, and he hated having the wardens sitting by him round the clock, watching his every move.

One day I was hauled into the office here and told he was being abusive, racist and actually violent to one of the wardens. That came as a huge shock: it was so unlike Ally, quite the opposite of how he used to be. He seemed to be turning into the sort of man that would once have disgusted him. I apologized on his behalf, said he just wasn't in his right mind, and told them they must be hard with him and tell him off if he misbehaved again.

To try to calm Ally down, I took over some of the supervision for a while: I did the 9am-till-11pm watch, and they took over between 11pm till 9am. At least he was doing well with his physiotherapy. He could stand in his standing frame for a full eight minutes now before his back started killing him and I had to lower him into his wheelchair again. The trouble was, he wouldn't stand just for me: he'd only do it to show his friends when they came to visit.

So if he'd been in his wheelchair for a long time and needed some standing practice, I'd ask Paul or Sandra to visit and then I'd say: 'Oh, show Paul how long you can stand for now, Ally,' or 'Show Sandra how you can stand, Ally,' and he'd happily submit to being strapped in the frame to perform for them. And I'd even bring him a cup of tea while he was standing up, to make him less self-conscious about the whole business. But no matter what I did, he hated me. I was being just as affectionate and loving as I was in normal life, and I was keeping him laughing, but he still didn't like me for it, which was heartbreaking.

I'd heard that one in three marriages didn't survive this stage, but I hadn't understood that until now. Day after day, I watched him with pride as he made progress – doing a new exercise, throwing a ball, reading a whole sentence of text without falling asleep, and even starting to walk with three people assisting him. It was so amazing it made me cry – but he wasn't my husband. He looked like him, smelled like him, and snored like him when he was asleep, but he just wasn't the same man.

I scared myself with the possibility that those frontal-lobe strokes had stripped away everything that I'd previously loved about Ally. It all seemed so horribly unfair. Surely, after all we'd been through, and after the miracle of Ally surviving such a devastating disaster, the story couldn't end like this, could it? Where was the 'happily ever after'?

CHAPTER 20

WHEN I spoke to Grace Maxwell about Edwyn's rehabilitation, I learned that Edwyn only started to feel and act like himself when he rediscovered his creativity and started bringing music back into his life.

So much of Ally's personality was bound up with his love of playing guitar, and there was a spark of hope here: if he started playing guitar again, maybe more of the old Ally would return to us. He hadn't shown much interest in the guitar so far. When the unit had suggested bringing in one of his guitars for some OT, he'd said he didn't want to play: he couldn't sit properly to hold the guitar, for one thing, because his muscles were still not up to the job. He had tendonitis in his right shoulder, so it was agony for him to use his right hand for strumming or picking the strings. There was also very likely a part of him that was fearful he wouldn't ever be able to play again – so attempting to play, and failing, would only be depressing for him. Maybe music would be too stressful for him now, I thought. I told him he could be a gardener instead, which was an idea he liked. Thinking about seeing his garden again, and what had grown there while he'd been in hospital all this time, seemed to be one thing that was giving him a yearning to return home.

There'd been periods in his life when he hadn't been that busy, and I noticed he'd be quite down at those times, so I knew he needed a sense of purpose every day. We just didn't know yet what would give him that sense of purpose. Before this had all happened, Ally had been working quite a lot with the musician and songwriter Matt Marsden.

Matt's wife Mel and I were already good friends after meeting in the music industry, and the four of us used to have tremendous fun together.

Weeks ago, Matt had gone into a music shop with a singer-songwriter he and Ally had been working with called Daisy Dares You, and on the wall of the shop was a very special instrument, a 1960 white National guitar. Ally had only been telling Matt a few days before how he loved the sound of

National guitars (which are American acoustic guitars that have metal resonators in the middle of the body) but that he didn't have one in his collection.

On the way home in the car, Matt and Daisy had said they should phone Ally that evening to tell him about it. But that was September 8, and instead they got a text saying that Ally was fighting for his life and it wasn't looking good. The very next morning, Matt returned to the shop, bought the guitar and then wrote on Ally's Facebook page 'I bought a white National guitar. Now wake up so we can play it together.'

After about eight weeks of rehab, on a day when Ally was showing no sign of enjoying anything except eating biscuits, I asked Matt to come in with his guitars. I thought he'd be the perfect person to give Ally guitar therapy: not only was he a good friend, but he was cool and laid-back and he shared Ally's passion for music and guitars.

So Matt turned up with the gorgeous 1960 National, as well as a 1963 Martin acoustic, and the unit gave them a private room and we let them get on with it.

Matt emerged after a short while, looking really happy, and said they'd played the old song 'Banks of the Ohio', and when they'd reached the middle part Ally had spontaneously started to play the guitar solo. He couldn't carry on playing for more than about 10 minutes, as it started to hurt and he was losing concentration. But it was a big moment: he'd proved he could still play! Mind you, I knew I'd have to keep reminding him about it, because he would soon forget Matt was ever here. But he could definitely still play guitar, and he wouldn't have to be afraid any more that he'd lost one of his most important abilities forever.

There was more progress to come. On Monday, December 7, Ally took his first steps by himself; he was in a frame, but he managed it without anyone holding him up. He wasn't falling down any more, so he came off 24-hour watch and got his privacy back, and he could get around the unit by standing behind his wheelchair and pushing it along. And, though he still had to be reminded to do it, he could now go to the loo by himself. Our dear friend and former neighbour Aida, from the hairdressers Scissors Palace in Holland Park, came to the unit and gave Ally a lovely haircut.

He was starting to care much more about his appearance now, getting dressed in his old clothes instead of staying in his pyjamas. He had his BlackBerry here, and one day when I popped out to buy his toiletries and food, I thought I'd try phoning him to see if he'd answer. I was so shocked when he did, all I could say was: 'Er... er... oh... er... Don't forget you've got physio in five minutes, hon!'

The home visit was looming now, and they said he'd have to come home in his wheelchair. So three ladies, including our social worker, came to the bungalow to see if any modifications would have to be made, like installing support rails in the bathroom.

Luckily, there was already a ramp at the side of our funny little building, so I could wheel him all the way up to the back door. This was the first time in four months that I'd been home in the daytime, and it felt weird. I had this overwhelming feeling that I should get back to Ally in hospital as soon as I could, despite the fact that I'd decided that now was a good time to back off and start giving him more time to himself. His brain and his body weren't on the same page yet.

One evening, Mum asked him how his standing was going, and he said he could do it, no problem, and got up from his wheelchair without using the standing frame. 'What are you doing, Al?' she said. 'You have to hold on!' Of course, he just fell back down again. 'It's weird, Pam,' he explained, 'my brain tells me I can do it, but my body says I can't. And I can't work out which one to listen to.'

He was still confabulating a lot – telling me he'd been swimming, for instance, which he hadn't. But I was seeing occasional flashes of his old sweet nature too. He asked me to go and buy a packet of crisps for Tony, because Tony had given him his last packet. I was sure Ally wouldn't have given a toss about that a week ago, but now he recognized Tony's generous gesture and wanted to return it.

Friday, December 11 became the big day when Ally would make his first short home visit. It was going to be just one night, but then I persuaded them to let him stay over on the Saturday and into Sunday morning. I told them that I was ready and it would all be fine, and if there was a problem, Dave was only round the corner and he could help.

On my way home from the unit at 11pm on the night before the visit, I motored down to the DIY store on Finchley Road and bought a beautiful real seven-foot-high Christmas tree, which I squished into my Smart Car. Somehow I got it into the bungalow, then got it standing up and looking gorgeous, with twinkling lights and the little angel I'd had for 20-odd years perched on top.

Standing there looking at it, I couldn't stop crying. Friday would be the first day of our new life, and I hoped it would go as I'd pictured it in my head. Ally and I would relax and laugh together, watch TV, play music, eat wonderful food, have friends over, and stargaze while wrapped up in our Scottish wool blankets – everything we'd done before in our gorgeous lives, but just a bit slower and with a wheelchair and a frame. I'd tried to build the visit up for Ally: 'You're coming home at the weekend, hon. Are you excited?' But I didn't get much reaction, and he'd forgotten all about it when the moment came to fetch him. He seemed to remember when I turned up with Steve and pointed out the window at Steve's big Range Rover outside, waiting to take him home.

Of course, our new home life was nothing like I'd pictured it. Ally didn't want to do anything except eat and sleep. When I put a DVD on so we could watch a film together, he couldn't concentrate and became uncomfortable and moany, and asked to go to bed. So I put him to bed, where he peed, despite the fact that he had a bottle to do it in; luckily, I'd anticipated this and bought some waterproof sheets.

He seemed angry with everything, and was stubbornly opting out of normal life. He didn't want to speak to his family on the phone, see little Rose, or even touch his guitars. When I took him back to rehab and everyone excitedly asked how it went, I told them it was great, we'd had a lovely time. I couldn't admit that I'd hated every second of it. Back at the unit, Ally got busy again with his OT. One task they'd set him was to search on the internet for a nearby bookshop, write down the address, try to get himself and his occupational therapist there using a map, and go in and buy a book. Good luck, I thought – he was always rubbish at directions! But they said he'd done really well, and now they were even trusting him to go to the shop downstairs, with his own money, to buy himself a magazine.

Meanwhile, in the outside world, the run-up to Christmas was in full swing. We've always loved Christmas in our family, and we do it big-style. I usually have a really warm glow at this time of year, and love spending loads of time with family and friends, having lovely food and playing endless games. But I was finding it hard to get my usual Christmas feeling. I got a little sprinkling of it every night, when I gave thanks to the big illuminated angel on top of the garden centre near my house. But I needed more, so I got involved with the Christmas party arrangements at the unit. It gave me a purpose that I'd been lacking since Ally had gone into rehab. I'd had a definite role when he'd been in critical and in the big ward after that, but now I was little more than the brunt of his frustration and anger. It was great that he was becoming more independent every day, but after he'd relied so heavily on me for all that time, it was really hard to come to terms with not being needed any more. I'd been made redundant, effectively. Well, nearly – I was still on toilet duty. Lucky me!

I needed to count my blessings, because it was absolutely no good both of us being depressed. When the time came for the Christmas party, Ally really wanted to stay in bed, though so many of our friends had come. They made him get up, but he didn't really enjoy himself – though he turned out to be useful when we had music and football questions in the quiz.

That night, I walked home in the snow with Sandra, and we made a pact to try to keep Ally laughing, to lighten his mood.

It was nearly time for Ally's Christmas home visit. We decided the family would celebrate Christmas at Karen and Dave's house rather than Mum and Dad's, which would be better for little Rose and much nearer for Ally. So I picked Ally up on Christmas Eve morning in the Smart Car – I did the journey on my own, to make sure I could cope by myself with all the heavy lifting. His wheelchair didn't quite fit in the back as it had in Steve's Range Rover, so I left it sticking out of the half-open boot, and put the heater on full.

Ally initially seemed a bit better than before: there were still no smiles or laughter, but at least he wasn't scowling at me all the time. When we got home, I ordered his favourite takeaway, chicken chow mein from the Chinese – but he hated it and immediately sank into a dark mood. It hadn't occurred to me that his personality changes would alter so many of the things he liked. How long would it take to discover what his NEW favourite takeaway was? What would his new favourite music be, and wouldn't I be his favourite person any more?

Christmas with the Pooles is usually a riot, and there were usually a few funny stories to treasure forever. Dad would do magic tricks and completely cock them up, or Mum would leave an important part of the dinner in the oven and only discover it when we'd finished. But there were no great memories this time: we were all too busy making allowances for Ally and pretending it was all normal and fun, when we all knew it wasn't. We'd all been building up to this moment, saying it was a momentous occasion, the day we never thought would happen. And once again it was a huge disappointment.

We made it through Christmas by the skin of our teeth, and then came New Year. I'd planned for some friends to come over on New Year's Eve, but Ally was in a terrible mood and didn't want to see anyone. We stayed in that night and Ally hardly said a word. Every time I tried to have a conversation or a cuddle with him, he just tutted and said he wanted to go back to the unit.

Our neighbours were celebrating the brand-new year with fireworks, and I asked Ally to come outside with me and watch the free light show, but he said he didn't want to. I went out on my own, but I could hardly see the fireworks for the tears in my eyes. I don't think I've ever cried so hard in my whole life. I turned away so there was no way he could see me out the window, because if he'd seen me it would only have made him mad. I looked up at the midnight sky and said 'It's not fucking fair!' It shouldn't be like this. We'd been given the biggest lesson of our lives and we'd worked so hard and come through it, learned what we'd had to learn.

Ally had survived against all the odds, it had been a bloody miracle – except it hadn't, because this wasn't my Ally any more, but a mean and nasty impostor; we'd lost the real Ally somewhere and now he was nowhere to be found. 'Please, please, please,' I asked, 'could I have him back?'

The entry I wrote in my diary on December 29 shows the full horror of that Christmas: *Today he was so mean, horrible. He said he'd had a horrible Christmas and that no one made any effort to accommodate him, that his parents don't even care that he's had a stroke, and that he'd have rather have been at the unit.*

I hate saying it but I seriously think i might have to leave him if he stays like this, he's not my Ally at all. I realize what's happened to him and that he's depressed and angry but he's not my Ally, he's someone completely different . This is very hard. How long do you do this for? He doesn't care for other people at all.

Spoke to unit again about husband's change in personality. They said it's very hard to say whether it comes back or not, but they want to be a support to us both, which is nice. I took Ally to Yo Sushi even though I wanted to chuck him under a bus. I sort of don't want to be in this any more, but then sometimes I look at him and remember who he was or see his face when he's sleeping and I can't not feel sorry for him. Even though he's nothing like the man he was, he still looks like him, which is soooo hard.

He has no thought for other humans right now. I've never known such a horror. I hope he comes back. I'll try everything. I've got to give it more time.

That was the last diary entry I wrote. I even got as far as phoning Brenda and saying I wasn't sure if I could cope with him when he came home, and he may have to come and live in Glasgow for a bit. That was a real option for a while. Anyway, by the end of week 9 he'd met all of his goals at the unit and he wanted out. He'd had enough and needed some privacy at home again.

I was sure he wasn't ready to come home, and I was so nervous about living with this man who'd once been my husband and was now a stranger, I wanted him to stay here. But he was adamant, so I gave in and signed him out. I knew I had some hard work ahead, but my family and friends were so thrilled for me, telling me how happy I must be. I couldn't tell anyone that I wasn't happy at all.

Back home, apart from showing definite personality changes, he was having all kinds of physical problems that didn't help his mood. As his body came back to life, he had pins and needles everywhere, and was very itchy in lots of places. He had astigmatism in his left eye and his left hand was quite shaky. It took ages for him to learn to go to the toilet properly, but he finally mastered that. He worked so bloody hard on himself in the next few weeks; he had such a drive to get back to normal again, and I hoped he really would be normal – that the real Ally would come back to me. The team in rehab advised that I get Ally to the doctor's when he left the unit, because while they'd worked hard on his brain, he had a lot of medical issues that were beyond the scope of rehab: things like his high heart rate and possible fibrillated arteries would have to be dealt with by his GP.

So he went off for some blood tests – he insisted on going alone, which I really shouldn't have let him do.

When he returned he was really happy and pleased with himself, but incredibly vague about the results. Asked what the blood tests had revealed, he replied: 'Er... they're all fine. They think I'm doing great and they aren't worried about anything.' 'Oh, you didn't ask, did you, you doofus?' I said. 'Yes I did,' he said. 'I'm all fine! Don't you trust me at all, Shell?'

Well, the short answer to that was no, because all the time he was brain-damaged I'd got used to him getting confused and doing ridiculous things, and it was going to take time for him to earn my trust all over again. So I booked another appointment straight away, and we were back at the doctor's about an hour later to hear the truth. And, sure enough, the doc went through his notes and said: 'Yes… blood pressure is still high… and oh, er, gosh! You have dangerously high cholesterol!'

So he was put on a high dose of simvastatin to combat the cholesterol, as well as a special diet with no fats, no salt and no sugar – nothing that he liked, in fact!

Since then he's been to regular checkups at the hospital, and each time the consultants couldn't conceal their amazement that this man was alive and walking and talking in their office. When I was close to finishing this book, I asked if I could go with him to his latest appointment, because I wanted to catch up with the experts' opinions on his health.

he consultant we saw was impressed with how well he looked, and asked how he was walking and managing stairs. 'Oh, I'm running a lot now,' said Ally, 'and I'm back at the gym. I'm doing a half-marathon in September…'

Slightly taken aback, the consultant then asked about his cognitive abilities; did he have any difficulties now? 'I don't think I have any,' said Ally, and the consultant gave me a look of concern, as if he thought Ally might still be severely brain-damaged and talking nonsense.

'I'm not sure he has any difficulties either,' I offered, adding that I thought Ally was basically 'back to normal'. The consultant swallowed hard and said: 'You know you're more likely to win the National Lottery than have an outcome like this?' And he went on to quote all the sorry statistics that we knew now by heart.

'Do you think we can actually use the word 'miracle' for what's happened to him?' I asked.

'In this case, madam,' the consultant replied, smiling, 'I think we could.' Medical experts not known for their hyperbolic language have used the phrase 'freak of nature' when referring to the strange case of Ally McErlaine and the subarachnoid haemorrhage that very nearly finished him off.

Reading his rehab reports recently, I spotted the phrase 'miraculous recovery' twice. And they were only talking about the rehab: that was after the other miracle, the one that allowed him to survive at all. And the biggest miracle, for me, is that my Ally – the wonderfully complicated but simple, intelligent but daft-as-a-brush husband – got his personality back, despite all the expert predictions that it wouldn't happen.

Every time Ally enquires who I'm meeting or what time I'll be home, or a text message pops up from him, I look up and say a massive thank-you, because I'd prayed for the day he cared about me again, the day I became his wife again. I'm so grateful that we can be normal once more.

fter he got his driving licence back, I stopped driving and let him get on with it, and I didn't feel the slightest bit guilty about that. I regularly load his arms with shopping bags now, telling him it's 'good physio'. I'd never use the word 'miracle' lightly, but I believe we have seen one here, a true miracle.

So how did it happen? Well, he had some of the best doctors and nurses in the world devoting months to caring for him, treating him and mending him in every possible way. My gratitude to everybody at the National Hospital for Neurology & Neurosurgery is too enormous to describe in mere words.

Then, of course, there was the amazing rainbow army, the network of men and women who ventured beyond medical science and harnessed powers that humanity still doesn't full understand.

I firmly believe that the vast amounts of positive energy we received from the visualizers, the crystal healers, the reiki practitioners, the people of all religions praying to God and the archangels, lighting candles and doing a myriad of other weird and wacky things, made a huge difference. How could it not?

I also think there's something unusually powerful about Ally's spirit: despite shocking brain damage and terrible odds, he simply refused to give up and leave this world. And he didn't stop there: he insisted on returning to normal, fighting to become Ally McErlaine again.

I refused to give up too, I was insanely greedy about getting him back 100%, so I have to accept that there may be something unusually powerful about my spirit too. Or perhaps we all have powerful spirits, but they're so rarely tested as cruelly as ours were. I know that I'd never fought so hard for something in my life before this. And I pray that I never have to again. Ally's still the deeply rational man he was before this all happened, and I thank God and the universe every day without him seeing or knowing, because he'd think I was nuts. I'm so thankful that everything ultimately happened in the order that it did. I've terrified myself by looking back at the whole story and asking myself: 'What would have happened if such-and-such was different, or so-and-so hadn't done what they did?' and a thousand other what-ifs.

The answer, I think, is that Ally might have died. For example, what if he'd had his haemorrhage just weeks earlier, when we were on holiday in Italy? What if he hadn't had it at home, but when he was out in the middle of nowhere, driving down a country road or taking photographs in a forest? What if he'd had it at home but I'd been out shopping or visiting friends, so I hadn't found him for hours?

Red Sky July finally made the album in Bristol, more than a year after we were just about to before Ally left us. Soon after Ally came home, our manager Jazz Summers said we should set a date because it would give Ally something to work up to. He had total faith that it would happen, and it was another turning point for Ally, because he fully became the musician he'd formerly been.

Ally, Charity and I recorded everything live in the studio with the rest of our band – Mark Neary, Paul Wigens and Dan Moore – with Rory Carlisle producing, and it was perfect. I knew it would happen, I just knew it, and I can honestly say it's the best work we've ever done. In the darkest days of Ally's adventure, I remember virtually renouncing music, imagining that it was now totally irrelevant my life. But making the album reminded us how much we love music, and what a massive part of our lives it is.

Christmas 2010 was amazing. Rose was so funny, and she absolutely adores her Uncle Ally. Dad did a 'rotating head' trick (don't ask) and Mum and I completely forgot the stuffing balls for the dinner. Ally grew a comedy moustache (oh, no, sorry, it wasn't meant to be funny) and dragged Karen's young stepdaughter Evie around in the snow on a toboggan. It was a proper Christmas, the one we'd been waiting for. But everyone who goes through a trauma like this has to heal in stages: psychologists tell you that from day one.

I thought I could be Superwoman and skip a few of those stages, but of course they're dead right: you get through each stage, one by one, with heightened emotions and massive highs and lows, and you can't heal any other way.

When things seemed to have calmed down, Dad and I both lost our singing voices for a while. Dad actually sounded strangulated when he tried to sing, as if there was an actual pair of hands wrapped round his neck. He had some vocal and breathing coaching, and now he's singing like a 16-year-old again. And now I'm back to singing and writing and finding it all fun again, but it's taken a while and considerable help from my lovely friends and colleagues who look after me (and take the piss out of me).

Ally still has absolutely no idea of the enormity of what he went through. He was so lucky that that part of his memory never came back. He has often laughed when I've described the tiniest parts of his drama to him, as if I'm fibbing or exaggerating wildly.

As I was writing this final chapter, Ally had his hands on my shoulders and was reading over my shoulder, and he saw the bit in my last diary entry where I say 'He has no thought for other humans right now. I've never known such a horror. I hope he comes back.'

'Oh no, Shell, don't tell them that! It makes it sound really bad,' he said. 'I wasn't really like that, was I?'

I handed him the diary. 'Read it, Ally,' I said. "I think it's time.'

Ally looks after himself much better than he ever did before. He regularly goes running, goes to the gym, and he even uses iPhone apps to monitor his heart rate and blood pressure. With all the cardiovascular nightmares he's been through, he still has to be careful about what he eats, and maybe I do nag him about his diet from time to time.

But his sense of humour is a wonderful antidote to all of that. When I went away for a few days in Norfolk, working on a musical project with our friend and co-songwriter Andy Hill, Ally sent a message to me on Facebook for all our friends to read and chuckle over. 'Come home, wife,' he wrote, 'there's only so much beer, sausages, chocolate and crisps I can take.' Hilarious!

I remembered to say a massive thank-you, and I had a bit of a cry-laugh, followed by a laugh-cry.

I still have the odd nightmare about all these traumatic events, and if Ally isn't in bed when I wake up, I worry and shout for him. But apart from that, it's as if it never happened; we've slipped back into normal happy life.

Ally doesn't like to talk too much about his terrible adventure, so it's been great therapy for me writing this book.

It's been like a good friend I can chat to and tell the truth to, and I've felt with every chapter I'm getting back to normal, like he did. To everyone who helped to bring Ally back, I dedicate this book. I can never thank you enough or send enough love back to you, but I'll endeavour to show my gratitude every day for the rest of my life.

THE END

Made in the USA
Charleston, SC
28 February 2012